Getting a W in the GAME of LIFE

Using My **T.E.A.M.** Model to Motivate, Elevate, and Be Great!

Dick VITALE

with Reji Laberje

ASCEND BOOKS

COUNTDOWN to tHe GaMe
Hear from the Successful People on Dickie V's TEAM

"Dick Vitale has shared his unsurpassed enthusiasm and passion with ESPN audiences for more than 30 years. He draws from a lifetime of experiences and a personal commitment to community service to provide an unforgettable motivational message."

George Bodenheimer, Executive Chairman of ESPN

"The first thing that stands out about Dick Vitale doesn't have anything to do with motivation at all. It is inspiration. Motivation is short-lived. He is one of the most inspirational human beings that I have ever personally encountered or witnessed, and I think a lot of people would agree with me on that. He brings a level of energy, enthusiasm and intensity along with smarts, know-how and ways to get ahead in this world, no matter what your circumstances are.

"Anybody that has an opportunity to listen to or read any of Dick Vitale's statements or words will be better for it instantaneously. The inspiration part is that you never forget what he has to say and it always moves you in a great direction. I am proof of that. I met him at a very young age, when he was the head coach of the Detroit Pistons, and will never forget how kind he was to me as a total stranger standing outside of the visitor's locker room at Tiger Stadium. It's moments like that when you never know when it's going to help shape you for the future, and that one did for me.

"Dick Vitale is a special, special person who has been reaching countless thousands of people for decades. This book will continue to build on all of those attributes that he carries with him and helps instill in people that he meets."

Tom Crean, Head Basketball Coach, Indiana University

"Dick is truly the eternal teacher. I see it every time I listen to him. As a 6th grade teacher and coach in the East Rutherford School District in NJ, Dick was forever the optimist, always encouraging his students to be the best that they could be. He sincerely believed that his students and players could achieve their dreams through dedication, enthusiasm and a positive attitude. A champion of the less fortunate, he always inspired through his passionate motivational talks. He was then, and still is, an "awesome" role model."

Lou Ravettine, Retired Principal, East Rutherford School District in NJ

"Over the last 20 years, I have been fortunate to hear Dick Vitale speak from the heart many times. His words are from the soul, delivered with great passion and depth, always inspiring us to push harder and reach higher. Your kids will love his inspiration as much as we love him!!!"
Mike Tirico, ESPN

"Dick Vitale has meant so much to so many people. He motivates me with all of the work he does for others, be it raising dollars for cancer research or telling kids to make good decisions in the game of life. I truly admire what Dickie V has done for others."
Rick Pitino, Head Basketball Coach University of Louisville

"In his early teaching days, Dick didn't just help kids with their basketball; he assisted them in getting into college or in finding other paths. Today, he does so much good for so many people that it makes one proud to know him."
Bob Stolarz, Retired Educator and High School Guidance Counselor

"Dick Vitale is still a kid at heart. He just happens to be one with the experience of being the best in his profession. He relates to the kid in all of us and to kids of all ages because anything he does is so genuine and appropriate."
Mike Krzyzewski, Duke University and
United States National Team Basketball Coach

"As a former athlete I have experienced all levels of motivation, but I didn't realize what real life motivation was until I met Dick Vitale. For 25+ years he has shown me what it takes to get the most…..No, EVERYTHING out of life….His passion for basketball has made him a Hall of Famer. His passion for life makes him much more….If you want an example of how to live life to the fullest…..Just read and learn!"
John Saunders, ESPN Broadcaster

"Dickie V is the ultimate motivator. Dick's passion and enthusiasm are unmatched in our game, whether you're talking coaches, his fellow broadcasters or students of the game. His love and work ethic make him a natural leader and a true inspiration. I only have to listen to Dick for a few minutes and I want to go out and be a better coach, a better leader and a better person."
John Calipari, Head Men's Basketball Coach, University of Kentucky

"Dick is an incredibly passionate person, and that shines through to everyone who comes in contact with him or reads his inspirational words."
Billy Donovan, Head Basketball Coach, University of Florida

10 9 8 7 6 5 4 3 2 1

ISBN: print book 978-0-9836952-9-5
ISBN: e-book 978-0-9856314-0-6
Library of Congress Cataloging-in-Publications Data Available Upon Request

Publisher: Bob Snodgrass
Publication Coordinator: Christine Drummond
Cover design, book design and illustrations: Rob Peters
Editor: Blake Hughes

Except where otherwise credited, photographs appearing in this book are from the personal collection of Dick Vitale.
Front Cover photo courtesy of John Atashian ESPN Images

Every reasonable attempt has been made to determine the ownership of copyright. Please notify the publisher of any erroneous credits or omissions, and corrections will be made to subsequent editions/future printings.

Printed in the United States of America

Dedications

I would like to dedicate this book to the gallant, valiant fighters I've met through the V Foundation for Cancer Research. It's through people like Payton Wright, Johnny Teis, Adrian Littlejohn, Duffy Alberta, Lucy Weber, Jothy Rosenberg, Mark Herzlich, Kurt Weiss, Jimmy Valvano and more whose stories I don't have enough pages to share, that I am motivated every day to help put an end to cancer. It is through their courage and bravery in the face of life's toughest struggle—the struggle for life—that I am elevated to keep the T.E.A.M. Model for not just a successful life, but a well-lived, good, positive life, in front of young people. It is because so many who were great lost their battles against cancer that I want to have the chance to make a difference for them. I think of these amazing fighters often. Some of them have stories of surviving and thriving. Others, even despite a winning attitude, lost the battle to cancer. Every one of them has enriched my life, and in their memories and honor it is my hope that this book will help enrich their cause as it raises awareness and dollars for the V Foundation for Cancer Research. To those out there who are still in the battle, "DON'T GIVE UP! DON'T EVER, EVER GIVE UP!" Your TEAM is working hard and my TEAM is too, with the strength of the memories of so many who have fought this fight before you.

Dick Vitale

I'd like to dedicate this book to Jen Lewerenz, my cousin who lost her battle to Ocular Melanoma in 2011. You fought the good fight and showed all of those around you what it meant to be a "happy girl." You are loved and missed.

Reji Laberje

Contents

THe PRe-GAMe

HOW RiCHie ViTALe BeCaMe DiCKie V

In the paint...

On the front of this book, you can see me having the time of my life and living the American Dream as I celebrated with high-spirited fans before calling a game on ESPN. I was feeling Awesome, Baby, with a Capital A! In the thirty-plus years I've had as an announcer with ESPN, I've been blessed to take part in celebrations of winning players, winning teams, and winning games. Because of the joy I experience routinely, I feel like I've never worked a day in my life even though I fill every day to capacity. I want you to have that same feeling—a winning feeling in a winning life!

Photo Courtesy Jon Gardiner, Duke Photography

Dick celebrates with fans before calling a game on ESPN.

People look at me and think that I was born with the win... the W... in the game of life. The truth is that a W is not something you're given; it's something you build and earn, and you can have it, too.

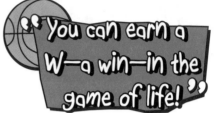

"You can earn a W—a win—in the game of life!"

I live every day with the same exuberance I feel when hanging with paint-faced fans, with players shooting from in the paint, or surfing on the hands of a crowd. It doesn't matter whether I'm calling a game, raising money to battle pediatric cancer through the V Foundation for Cancer Research, offering a hand to local Boys & Girls Clubs of America, speaking at corporate events, or living my life as a husband, a dad, and a grandfather. The passion I feel today is the same that I felt as a kid chasing my dream of being a basketball coach, starting out as a teacher, as a high school basketball coach reaching my goal of coaching at the college level, and even surpassing it by coaching in the NBA. It has been an absolute thrill to be a scholastic, collegiate, and NBA mentor! I wasn't always Dickie V, the ESPN sports broadcaster, but it was because of being full of passion for life that I was given the chance to become him.

Dick enjoys calling a game for ESPN.

Five-star Garfinkel...

I was coaching at East Rutherford High School in New Jersey when I met the man who would one day change my life. Howard "Five-Star" Garfinkel, "Howie", ran the Five-Star Basketball Camp, a prestigious camp for the best-of-the-best high school basketball players. Michael Jordan of college and NBA fame said the camp forever changed the way he looked at basketball. College coaches would look to Howie for his opinions on the hottest up-and-coming stars.

When I met Howie, it was right after our high school team became state champs in basketball. He came to the banquet and watched me introduce my incredible team. **I didn't know until later how that moment of just being myself and enjoying the night would affect my entire life.**

Recently, Garfinkel gave an interview to George Raveling, a former basketball coach. In it, I was so honored to hear him talk about that moment of meeting me. Howie told George, "For an hour, with no notes, he went on and on about his team and about every player. It was the most incredible thing I'd ever witnessed."

Garfinkel told me after that night that I was wasting my time in high school. I belonged in college. I loved my high school teaching and coaching job, but college? **That was the dream!** Even though I told him I had a stack of rejections, Howie called his friend, Dick Lloyd, who had just been named head coach at Rutgers University.

Dick and Howard Garfinkel.

"He can come," Dick told him, "but I've already got my choices. Zero chance I'm going to hire this guy," he told Howie. "I'll only talk to him as a favor to you." As you'll learn later in this book, **zero chances only come from zero attempts.** Not only did Dick Lloyd meet with me, he hired me within hours of the interview! He gave me a chance and suddenly I wasn't Richie anymore. I was Dickie V, and I was on my way to earning a W in the game of life.

Your turn...

I want you to make your dreams come true, too. I don't mean just dreams in basketball or broadcasting; those were my goals. I want to help you climb a ladder of success toward the dreams and goals you have for every part of your life. I want you to capture your dreams in education, the corporate world, the arts, or anything else you set your heart  and mind on making come true. I did it by being myself. You can do it by being your best self, too. **You're going to learn how passion, intelligent decisions, and hard work will equal success in your life!**

Throughout this book, I won't just tell you the stories of the successful people I've known throughout my life, I'm going to tell you how they got there. **You need inspiration? These are real life stories of real people!**

Everybody's success stories are told through the people around them... through their life TEAMs... and at the end of this book, I want to be a part of yours. You will learn that the T.E.A.M. Model is about the people in your life you've discovered, respected, and grown close to through TOGETHERNESS. It's about the ENTHUSIASM you *choose* every day and in every circumstance. It's about the ATTITUDE you reflect in every choice you make.

It's about having MENTAL TOUGHNESS to keep you strong when you're on top of the world as well as when you're facing adversity.

Through this playbook for the game of life, we will be a TEAM today!

Just as I use the real lives and words of heroes to motivate and elevate me toward greatness every day, I want to share those pieces of inspiration with you. You'll find notes from my M-File (M for Motivation) scattered throughout these pages.

Sometimes, it's a quote for you to reflect on. Other times, you'll hear the tales of *my* heroes, my favorite players, and the success tips passed on to me throughout my career and life. **You may be surprised to discover that there are a whole lot more people on my TEAM than the great basketball players I've been lucky to know over the years.** All of their names are also listed in my TEAM roster at the end of the book.

Also enjoy the exercises, the tear-out activities, and the questions that will help you to build your own T.E.A.M. Model for success, no matter what your goal is. I don't want to just give you the life tips I've learned, I want you to learn how to apply them and be motivated by them to elevate you toward your goal—elevate you toward greatness!

If you get a little lost, check out Dickie V's DicKtionary at the back of the book for a glossary of terms and "Vitalese" you may not recognize.  *From Dickie V's DicKtionary. That's also where you'll find the index of topics ranging from bullying, goal-setting, handling crazy schedules, and making life's most difficult decisions.

These indexed topics are what young men and young ladies discussed and showed concern for when this book was coming together. Their names have been changed, but you can see their thoughts in my "straight shooter" segments throughout the following pages. I

even have a playbook following each book section so that you'll have a map to lead you up your ladder of success and on the path toward being motivated, elevated, and great.

You're gonna be Awesome, Baby, with a Capital A!

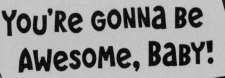
You're Gonna Be Awesome, Baby!

The T.E.A.M. Model

Togetherness—Learn about the relationships necessary to meeting your goals, making those relationships, and setting those goals. You'll also find out how to keep your most important friendships through thick and thin and how to manage your relationships in a world that runs on social media.

Enthusiasm—Discover the power of positive living at every stage of life, of giving back to your world, and of defining who you are to those who would put you in the middle of the gossip mill.

Use this bookmark to keep track of your place while you work your way through "Getting a W in the Game of Life"!

T
E
A
R

O
U

T

A

C

T
I
V
I
T
Y

Togetherness
- *Criticism comes from love.*
- *Friendships grow, but don't have to go.*
- *Facing Facebook.*

Enthusiasm
- *Define… Don't Defend.*
- *Schedule Your Success.*
- *Be a Millionaire of LIFE.*

Attitude
- *Be Good to People—They'll Be Good to You.*
- *Accountability, Responsibility, and Maturity.*
- *Never Believe in Can't.*

Mental Toughness
- *Winner's Edge or Quitter's Edge.*
- *Turning Discipline into Dreams.*
- *Beauty and the Bully.*

"You're gonna be Awesome, Baby, with a Capital A!"

Dick Vitale

TEAR. OUT. ACTIVITY

Attitude—Find out about the effects of respect for all people, accountability in your decisions, and a "never give up" attitude. In addition, read about people who have made bad decisions that brought them to the edge and then fought their way back through right living.

Mental Toughness—Study the mental work *and* the physical work of trying to meet your goals. Learn to defend against bullying in all of its forms, including your own thought process. Build your self-esteem in order to have the ultimate strong foundation to support your own T.E.A.M. Model for success.

TOGETHERNESS

From Dickie V's DicKtionary: *Togetherness is when people function and work as a team; it is a blending of people of different races, beliefs, and backgrounds. Life is about the people you connect with. If you can't get together with all kinds of different people, you're in a lot of trouble. You'll be a success when you accept people's differences and learn to experience togetherness.*

CRiTiCiSM COMES FROM LOVE; THANK GOD SOMEBODY CARES!

It starts at home...

I'm in eleven halls of fame. Eleven! You're crazy if you think I got there on my own. Nobody, I mean nobody, gets to the hall of fame alone. **Anybody who thinks they did it alone forgot how they really got there.** If you're in the Baseball Hall of Fame, somebody taught you as a kid how to hold a bat, how to stand, how to catch, and how to hit. You weren't born knowing how to do those things. You didn't get better at those skills without a coach or a buddy teaching you a few things. Nobody gets there alone.

I remember when future NBA great David Robinson went to the Naval Academy. He wasn't the top high school basketball player, but he worked and worked and worked and became the national player of the year, Baby! When he got the award, appearing in Navy dress blues and looking like a million dollars, he thanked his parents for taking him to little league, to computer classes, and to all of the things that added up to him growing into a man. He thanked them because it was every single bit of hard work and knowledge he had along the way that led him toward the goals he achieved.

David Robinson never forgot where he came from. Now his own son is going to Notre Dame on a football scholarship with the same principles that David passed along—the principles and values from his own parents: **pride, passion, and work ethic.**

I remember Hall of Fame basketball coach Bobby Knight sitting next to me at the Naismith Tip-Off Banquet. The celebration was to honor David Robinson of Navy as the Player of the Year and Coach Bobby Knight, "The General"— who had once coached the Naval Academy rival at West Point but was with Indiana at the time of this honor—as the Coach of the Year.

David Robinson of the Naval Academy basketball team.

Coach Knight leaned over and whispered in my ear, "Now, how would you like to coach that?"

David was a likable, admirable, coachable young guy. He handled criticism and worked with it to become a better player. He became the best in the nation. Too many people take criticism the wrong way instead of realizing that somebody may be critical because somebody cares.

When you're ready to make your own Hall of Fame in *life*, you need to find those people who are going to help you get there. Maybe you've got a great coach or teacher; you might build your TEAM from your community and the groups you belong to, or maybe you have brothers, sisters, or friends who will help. For me, my TEAM began at home.

Before I was Dickie V, I was just this young kid chasing a dream—chasing a goal, but it really started in a great home with great parents. While circumstances have changed for me, I have never changed in my heart. I have told my family to bring me back to reality if I ever think I'm better than anyone else.

I often tell people about my mom and dad, Mae and John Vitale. My parents were intelligent, hard-working, loving people. They weren't highly educated, but what they lacked in schooling they had in wisdom; wisdom of the heart. **They only had a fifth grade education, but they had doctorates in love.**

Dick with parents, John and Mae Vitale.

The dinner table with my folks was filled with even more life lessons than my years of education. I learned more around my dinner table from my mom and dad than from any class I ever took, and I took a lot of classes.

I learned about loyalty. I learned about adversity. I learned about family. My sister Terry, and brother John, were also a vital part of my life. These people, my family, were Hall-of-Famers in life and, from them, I learned about love. That love helped me in life; it still helps me in life. I felt like a millionaire growing up in that home.

Moms and dads are people, too...

I know that many of today's families are a lot more complicated.

Taylor had this to say:

"*My parents are divorced. I'm sick of seeing my parents fight. They're in a rivalry with each other. They're always competing. It's like I feel bad because if I say I love one of them, the other one feels like I'm putting them down."*

All I can say is… thank God you've got somebody who cares! Taylor, parents sometimes have to learn from us as much as we have to learn from them and they don't always communicate perfectly. They're human. We sometimes have to remind ourselves of this when it comes to the adults in our lives.

Before basketball, I had a real love for baseball, still do. I remember one game I was playing for my team sponsored by *Mazzo Oil*. I was on my way to pitching a no-hitter. My Uncles Tom Scarpa and Frank Scarpa were there watching the game. I wanted a  no-hitter badly, but with two outs in the last inning, the batter hit a groundball that went by the first baseman. The scorekeeper gave him a hit. Still, Uncle Tom and Uncle Frank emphatically loved the game, loved me, and were disappointed and upset that it was a hit when they felt it should have been an error.

My uncles didn't turn into over-the-top spectators who disrespect the game, the coaches, or their kids. Their enthusiasm for me and for the play simply spilled over. So many times today, parents get outrageous and demonstrate poor sportsmanship. Anything done on the field is ruined when that happens. This was different.

"That's a no-hitter," my uncles insisted, but they weren't arguing with anger. It was a debate. **They were arguing with love.** I could feel that. They both wanted to be the guy that helped me feel good. The call stood, but my uncles had wanted me to have a no-hitter and earn that W for my pride.

Even as a kid who was wrapped up in sports, I knew that role models should begin at home. Athletes are great to look up to for their skills and their talents, but it is the people who are filled with love who should be our role models, people like my uncles. (Even when they argue against a call).

OFFeNSive StRateGy
Recognize Love

My uncles are all gone now. They were part of my TEAM. I wish I could have them all back to say, "I love you." **"I love you" is not used enough today**. You would be amazed at how much those words can break up negativity. Don't ever let somebody stop you from saying those most important words to the most important people in your life.

Taylor and other kids in her situation don't have it easy. **Nobody wants to be around that negativity.** But they do have a choice. They can listen to the fighting and let it drag them down, or they can choose to recognize the love and be grateful that, even when their parents might be arguing, that arguing could be done out of love. Focus on the positive.

It's hard to see the pain these families endure when a marriage ends. My heart goes out to the kids. As an elementary school teacher, it was  one of the most difficult situations we faced. Sometimes a student would be stressed out, saying he hadn't gotten his work done because the house was full of yelling. I'd tell him the same thing then that I say today. **You can't blame yourself.** You have to let go and move on. You can't always control the scenario. With the oath of "I do," comes great responsibility, and even the best of people don't always make it. It's not a judgment. Young people don't always understand the difficulty of relationships and of surviving in homes filled with tension. Divorce happens. At the end of the day, do you still have a mom? A dad? They are still available to you in some way, and just like my student in a stressful situation, you'll be okay.

It's not just in the arguing, it's even in the criticism that a positive message has been known to hide.

Take what Derek had to say:

"My parents get on my back about being on the computer too much. They didn't even have computers when they were in school. They don't get it. They're afraid if I spend too much time on the computer, my grades won't be good. Enough with the grades! We get it. I'm just taking a break and most of my homework needs the computer anyway. Can't they just leave it alone?"

Maybe their approach is frustrating, Derek, but they can't just leave the issues alone. Our parents sometimes see better people in us than we see in ourselves—it's not just about the grades. Whenever I got down as a kid because of my eye injury, something I'll share with you later in these pages, my mother used to say to me, "Richie, nobody's gonna feel sorry for you just because you lost your eye." She knew that there were greater difficulties to overcome than my eye.

Believe me, this is exactly what "criticism comes from love" is all about! When parents are asking about school, your personal life and your activities, they're showing you that they care about you. Not all people have this love in their lives. **Be grateful.** Whether it's from a coach, a parent, or a teacher, you should feel good when you're receiving constructive criticism.

If you don't have a person in your life who is providing that positive criticism, the truth is that you need to find him or her. **Who can help you to be your best?** Maybe your relationship with your parents is strained. If so, find people you respect in your communities, your church, your school, in your activities, clubs, teams, or through organizations like the Boys & Girls Clubs of America, YMCA, or recreation departments. It's less important how you make those connections than it is that they are quality connections. It may not always feel like it, but somebody who pushes you is a good thing.

"Somebody who pushes you is a good thing."

There have been times in my life when I would have stalled out if it weren't for a push from my parents or my wife. We need that! Find people you respect, people with positive goals, and people headed in the right direction who are spending their time actively.

Are people like Derek upset that they are being asked to change a habit, or are they afraid of just how much they could do if they broke that habit? Are they afraid of change? **We choose our direction in life!**

When you're in school, you've still got youth, you've got choices, and you've got your whole life before you. It's an empty scoreboard and the shots you can take and make are countless. What would happen if you took the criticism of those who love you? Could you do more? Could you find new passions? **Could you be your best you...** because that's who your parents and loved ones see. That's who they know could be realized if you make intelligent decisions. Make it a goal to take that criticism and see how it could change you for the better.

Defensive Strategy

Evaluate Criticism

You have to remember who's on your TEAM. When loved ones fight, remember that they're just as human as you. When they criticize, think about why they might be telling you a different way to live or a different way to approach the day. If you're talking about parents, teachers, or coaches, chances are they're talking about helping you be your best.

Sunday morning uncles...

Let me tell you a little more about my TEAM, my folks, and the uncles who were at the start of my ladder of success. Sunday mornings were the usual gathering days. After church, Mom would have a big breakfast out on the table and they would all come over. This was the one day of the week for these real

American guys to take a break. They weren't educated by today's standards, but they were bust-your-gut, work in the factories, provide for your families kind of guys.

They would come by... and that's when the fighting would start.

"Who's better?" they'd say. "Willie Mays, Mickey Mantle, or Joe DiMaggio?"

I loved Willie Mays. My uncles liked Mickey Mantle. My dad said, "You guys have no idea what you're talking about, because the greatest of them all is Joe DiMaggio."

My uncles were peaceable men; they were just extremely passionate about sports. It was an unbelievable experience to be around them, and I developed a love for sports, a love for people, and a great love for how my family lived. **They weren't materialistic; they were just about love.**

I meant it when I said you don't get to the Hall of Fame alone. My uncles enthusiastically expressed their love of sports to me, dad and mom, and to one

"I developed a love for sports and a love for people."

another. It was the beginning of my journey to sports broadcasting with ESPN. When they dished the rock* of their enthusiasm to me, it set me up for my future of working with athletic greats.

*From Dickie V's DicKtionary

Dish the Rock - a "Vitalese" term; pass the ball.

FROM tHe

M FiLe

M FOR Motivation!

"Anytime you see a turtle on top of a fence post, you know he had some help."

~Alex Haley

My help was not just present in my family. I've been lucky to meet some great people in my career of calling basketball games, too... some real PTPers*!

One group of young guys in particular represented what it means to be a team. In 2006, the Florida Gators took the NCAA championship against UCLA. Three of these guys were just sophomores! Joakim Noah, Corey Brewer, and Al Horford were sitting on top of the world. It was no surprise that the NBA came calling. They came calling with fame; they came calling with fortune; they came calling with futures for these Florida players. Nobody would have blamed them for going. What an offer it was for these young guys to resist.

*From Dickie V's DicKtionary

PTPer - a "Vitalese" term; Prime-Time Player; a player of great basketball skill.

But they did resist! They wanted to make more than money—they wanted to make history! **I always tell people, "Do what you love; the money will come."** Not only did Brewer, Noah, and Horford return to the Gators, but so did Coach Billy Donovan, who was courted by Kentucky! These guys didn't want to mess with happiness. In 2007, the Gators became the first team to have the same starting five win back-to-back National Championships, this time against Ohio State. They also became the first school to hold Division I championship titles in football and basketball at the same time. Giving up that early career start was a tough decision, but for that choice, these Gators are the **PTPers of *Togetherness*!**

FRIENDSHIPS GROW,
BUT DON'T HAVE TO GO;
MOVING ON, GROWING UP, AND
KEEPING CLOSE.

From family to friends...

Our family might be our first teammates. Our childhood homes may be our first home courts, but the game of life is always changing. **We've all got to grow up.** New players come into our lives, new venues become our courts, and new strategies come into play.

When fans see me calling games all over the country, they often ask me, "Dickie V., how do you do it, man?"

It wasn't always like this. I lived in New Jersey for most of my life—grew up there, taught there, coached there, and met my wife, Lorraine, there. When I moved from New Jersey, where I'd lived for thirty-two years, I'd never

even been on a plane! I got the job at the University of Detroit and it was a real change for me—not just with my job, but emotionally. I had to leave family and I had to leave folks that had been a vital part of my life for so many years.

I found out one thing. **People are people wherever you live.** If you communicate and develop friendships and you're warm and caring with people, they will respond to you the same way wherever you are. I moved. I left a lot of people I was really close with.

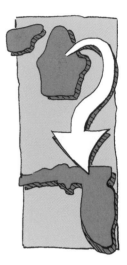

Later, with my wife and two daughters, we left Michigan and made Florida our home. If anything, we developed a bigger base of friends. People we knew from Jersey, from Michigan, and people we knew from my career on the road all came to visit us in Florida, and still do!

The truth is we all live in a world that is always moving, but we also live in a world that is more connected than ever. It's up to us to choose how we handle those moves. You can't use moving as a negative; you have to focus on the positive. In today's world, with all of the technology we have, you can continue relationships. **Communicate.** Correspond. Many times, moving becomes an excuse for breaking off a friendship. You can continue that relationship through means other than seeing that person every day.

Just because your place in the world changes doesn't mean your personality in it does. **Your relationships don't have to be attached to just one point in time**; they can be attached to you, to who you are, to what you know, and to your lifetime TEAM!

"Your place in the world may change, but your personality in it doesn't have to."

Let's deal with what Carlos has to handle:

"My dad is in the Army. If I'm lucky, I get to live in the same place for three years. Sometimes, though, I'm in a different school twice in the same year. I don't even bother trying to make friends anymore."

The worst thing you could do in a situation like Carlos' is to stop trying to connect. **We are incomplete without connections!** I remember how hard it was to move from New Jersey, where I'd lived my whole life, to Detroit, where I didn't know anybody. But when I moved away from those people, I was still me. I didn't lose the people I'd known all of my life. They were already on my TEAM.

Bob Stolarz at East Rutherford High School, 1971.

One of my greatest friends in New Jersey was Bob Stolarz. We knew each other from our school days. I was a sophomore playing basketball at Garfield High School and Bob, an eighth grader at the time, came to a lot of the games. We became friends because of our common interests in athletics, but this was just the beginning of our relationship. As adults, we were both teachers *and* he played a huge part in my growing into the role of coach at East Rutherford High School. He coached junior varsity and also helped me out with the varsity team.

We're still friends today! We're friends because he's bright, loyal, efficient, and never envious. He never wanted to hold me back from reaching my goals. He was content doing his job... and doing it well. None of these things changed when I changed my address. He took over coaching at East Rutherford after I left for Rutgers, and when I moved away and he moved up his own ladder, we were the same people we had always been. We keep in touch to this day. We see one another at family functions, occasional athletic functions, and whenever I'm in the Jersey area. We talk, we share, and we never forget who we are, where we come from, and how we're connected. He knew that I wasn't changing my core just because I was changing my zip code. The distance that separates us only makes visits and contact time more special, treasured, and appreciated.

In Detroit, after my seasons at Rutgers, it was time to recruit new members to my lifetime TEAM and still keep my starting lineup... still keep people like Bob Stolarz.

Today, more than ever, it is your own choice to stay in touch. We still have letters, but we also have the internet, cell phones, and video phones on our computers. **Losing touch is a choice... keeping in touch can be, too.**

Do you want to know what the TEAM you left behind has been up to? Ask. They'll feel good and you'll feel great. When we keep these connections alive, it keeps our spirits alive. It keeps our spirits up. You will be a stronger person if you learn to maintain relationships through all kinds of adversity, including distance.

DEFENSIVE STRATEGY
Don't Be A Recluse

Recruiting...

It's not only when you move, like Carlos, that you find your-self looking to put together a new group of friends, a new TEAM. Sometimes, moving on from your earliest connections happens as you get older because you try new things and find new people with whom to do those new things.

This is how Stephanie sees things:

"All of my friends are changing. Now, I'm friends with the people I do the same things with, like band. But, I still want my old friends. They're moving on with other people, too. I kind of feel left out. Sometimes my new friends are still close with their old friends, so I feel left out from them, too. I can't even tell who's in my circle."

Stephanie, you're not alone, and what I tell others who feel these same things is that it's just as important to make new relationships as it is to keep in touch with your first relationships. **You're changing.** You have new interests. You do new things. You should expect that your childhood friends have new interests, too. Keep in contact with them. Ask them what they're up to.

At the same time you reach back, remember to reach out! Invite new people over, and when they come, don't just share about you. Find out about them. What interests them? What do they do in their free time? Get to know their families. **Learn about the people you want to socialize with.** You'd want the same from them. Be the first to make that move. If you're connecting with a friend for the first time, then you'll be a lot more exciting to be around if you can share something that the person is enthusiastic about. Sports? Music? Art? Learn about what excites the other person so that *you* can excite the other person!

When you reach out, you don't always get a response right away, but keep trying. Keep communicating! And if somebody else is reaching out to you, answer the call. They're trying to do the same thing as you… **connect.**

OFFeNSive StRateGY

Reach Back AND Reach Out

The important thing to remember is that you're not the only one who finds herself in the position of having to deal with changing relationships. You can keep your early friendships and you can grow new ones at the same time. At every stage of your life, you will have relationships that become a part of your TEAM, that make you a better person, that you can help toward their goals, and that can help you up your own ladder of success.

GAME TIPS!
Remember...

Stay Connected with Your First TEAM.

Expand your Horizons with a New TEAM.

Life is about people...

When I worked in Detroit and still had close friends in New Jersey, I was meeting, getting to know, and making lifelong relationships with people who became necessary to the next steps in my life journey.

After coaching college ball at the University of Detroit, I was moving on to the NBA. It was the last game I would be coaching in college, so I'd flown my uncles in for the game. They were so proud. We had just won 21 in a row, including beating Al McGuire's great Marquette team, the team that won the national title later that year. What a feeling it was to beat Marquette on their home court in Milwaukee. The University of Detroit Titans team was good. We were more than good. We made it to the Sweet 16* and we

*From Dickie V's DicKtionary

Sweet 16 – In college basketball, Sweet 16 refers to the top sixteen teams that are fighting their way toward the NCAA championship title game in a bracket-style elimination playoff.

were getting to play the one team we'd always wanted to play... Michigan.

The whole state was in a frenzy. The players were ecstatic because all they had ever heard about was Michigan, Michigan, Michigan; now was their chance to get them all shouting Detroit, Detroit, Detroit. City-on-state, neighbor-on-neighbor—this was the match-up my team had been begging for—an underdog against the big dogs. The importance of this game didn't go unnoticed by the national media.

The night before the game, we went to Rupp Arena in Lexington, Kentucky, where the tournament was being held. The place was nearly empty except for three guys sitting in the stands. I couldn't believe it. Sitting there were some of the all-time greatest names in the game: Coach John Wooden, sportscaster Curt Gowdy, and a man I didn't know, but was about to hear. As we were getting ready to practice, I brought my team over to meet these legends, and the third guy introduced himself.

"Hi, Dick. My name is Scotty Connal. NBC is broadcasting the game tonight in the Midwest."

I was at the end of my career in college and the beginning of my journey in the pros. I could have worried about the changes coming in my life. I could have stood still and decided that I had enough friends. I was about to be a coach in the NBA for the Detroit Pistons. I didn't need the hassle of new relationships. That's not the advice I give people because that's not what I believe.

I was glad to meet new people. I was open and friendly. Then I had my pre-game talk and got ready for the game. I was being true to myself and never afraid of reaching out to meet somebody new.

It wouldn't be a major story if, two years later, I hadn't gotten fired from the NBA. About a week after losing that job, my phone rang. It was Scotty.

"Hi Dick," he said. "You probably don't remember me, but in 1977 I was there when you played the game against Michigan and I heard you talk to your team. I am in charge of production for a new network called ESPN. We were wondering if you would like to broadcast our first basketball game between DePaul and Wisconsin."

I didn't take the job right away, but I did shortly after. That call changed everything. **If I hadn't decided to extend a hand on that day in 1977, Scotty might not have extended the offer that reshaped my life.** You never know how and when your life can change. I didn't know it at the time, but I was always networking, meeting the people around me, being myself, and sharing with others. Don't ever, ever close the door to new friends, new acquaintances, and new people in your life.

FROM tHe M File

M FOR Motivation!

"Extend a hand with love in your heart, and people will give you love in return."

~John Wooden

DiCkie Do's aND DoN'ts!

DO...	DON'T...
Send a handwritten note to old friends, asking how they are.	Assume that your friends have forgotten you because you've moved.
Learn about the interests of new friends.	Spend all of your time talking about yourself.
Invite new and old friends to your home or out for social gatherings.	Be afraid of meeting the other friends and family of new people in your life.
Celebrate the special events of friends and loved ones.	Be so caught up in yourself that you disconnect from others.
Keep communicating using letters, email, phone, and video chatting.	Ignore the calls of new and old friends who may be trying to reach out to you.
Make new relationships wherever you are in your life.	Cut yourself off from possible new friendships because of a concern of one day moving on from them.
Be yourself in all relationships.	Fear making the first move.

FACING FACEBOOK;
NAVIGATING RELATIONSHIPS IN THE
WORLD OF SOCIAL MEDIA.

From friends to friend lists...

Every week I read another story about something being put up on a web page with terrible results: pictures taken in locker rooms, texts sent that were supposed to be personal, and status updates or tweets being shared without thinking about who those thoughts might affect. Kids are hurting each other mentally, spiritually, and even physically with these technologies that were meant to make us closer. Remember what I said. Life is about people. We need face-to-face connections, not just interface connections.

If you want to make it today, you need to stay on top of the world of technology. So, how do you deal? How do you balance social media with social consequences?

How do we help people like Ashley:

"When I opened an account on Facebook, I added my classmates. I like to know what's going on and sometimes that's how everybody invites people to parties or nights out. One of my classmates kept posting all sorts of stuff on my wall. Because of the stories, my parents got mad. Sometimes this guy would start swearing at my friends and they'd get upset with me. It's not my fault. I'm not the one who said or posted those things."

Ashley, we're all discovering how to use the new online worlds we live in. I had a fan that followed me on Twitter. I can't keep track of all the followers I have, but this one guy stood out. He had a mouth on him. He constantly posted things that were full of foul words. I wasn't the guy using unacceptable language, putting down players, cussing out coaches, or offending followers. **But my name was on the top of that page. That page—whether I write it or not—shows people who I am.**

I admit that I didn't know about it then, but you can block people. I took this person off my list and let him know that that type of talk

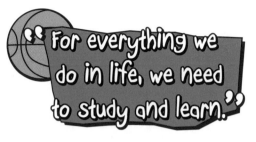

"For everything we do in life, we need to study and learn."

wasn't okay. I've taken the time to learn since then what tools are available. For everything we do in life, we need to study and learn—why not do the same when you're online?

Learn about the privacy, the protections, and the ways to make your web presence reflect your character. Like it or not, we're judged by what's out there about us. It's our job, in today's connected world, to have the knowledge and the skills to be our best selves in the cyber world, too.

DEFENSIVE STRATEGY
Learn the Tools

Consider the source...

The cyber world hasn't just changed the skills we need, it's changed the friends we have. In fact, it's even changed the definition of the word 'friend'. Since when did putting a name on a list make you feel really connected to that person? You're on a list of all of the students in your school. Does that mean you're close with all of them? No way! If you're in a big school, you probably don't even know everybody on that list. Why do people forget this when they are in front of their keyboards or the touch screens of their phones and smart pads?

See what Will shared:

> *"I belong to a group page online. It's for all of the kids that do any sports in our school, so we don't all know each other. We sometimes talk about equipment or other things, though. It's like a forum. This guy commented on a picture I put up of a new pair of shoes and said that my rich parents probably got them for me. He doesn't even know me! I work and my parents don't spoil me."*

If you don't know the person, he doesn't know you, either. Sometimes, because we belong to a certain club or group, we end up with people on our friend lists or pages who we don't personally know. Will, you can't be upset by somebody who doesn't know you. If you are in a public group and you can't control what people say, this is the only thing you'll have to remember to keep from being brought down by negativity.

You can't be personally upset by someone who doesn't personally know you.

I learned this lesson when I shared my thoughts about a professional basketball player who had been suspended for several games because he had gotten rough on the court. There's no need for that! It's despicable. That's not what the game is about. A disgruntled fan of mine commented on my page that I would never say these things to the player's face. All I realized was that this man didn't know me. Isn't this true when it comes to many of our online relationships?

You can have online connections, but don't confuse them with the sort of relationships you build by knowing a person in real life, away from the computers, keyboards, and the smart phones. **Know the difference between a friend and a friend list.**

Oversharing and undersharing...

You know we have tools to be safe online. You know we have friends that aren't the same as our friend lists. Still, young people (and their parents) keep putting their whole lives out there with phones and computers. It takes away from our privacy, from our real relationships, and from what makes **the most memorable moments** of our lives special.

I don't post every picture I have with my friends, my wife, my children, and my grandchildren. I did once post a wonderful family highlight, a personal joy, only to receive

FROM the M FiLe

M FOR MotivatioN!

"If we take care of the moments, the years will take care of themselves."

~Marie Edgeworth

an unwelcome comment from an unknown stranger. I felt like he had invaded my privacy and taken away from a great memory I was having with a loved one.

What if you have friends who aren't online? How would they feel if all sorts of people you knew from a website were finding out about important things in your life before they did? How would you feel finding out about a great moment in a friend's life from a public posting? When you have a picture, a thought, a great idea or a memory, share those things in person with your friends or family. Pull that picture up on your phone and show your loved one or teammate the shot while you're at lunch or when you're hang-ing out. Share your joy with those who bring you joy. **They will feel like they know you a little better**

"Share your joy with those who bring you joy."

because you are sharing something face-to-face with them.

If you do choose to put anything on the internet or in a text on your phone, you need to realize that once you hit "send," you could be sending to the whole world.

When I come home after a speaking engagement, a game, or a fundraiser the first thing I do is go to my office and write a thank you note. I show my appreciation, share my joy, and keep the connection alive. I'm not saying we shouldn't communicate with the tools we have today, but **nothing makes you feel better than making somebody else feel good**. Nothing does a better job of that than heartfelt words on a handwritten note.

Awesome, Baby with a Capital A!

I had the thrill of my life being a part of a special Veteran's Day event in 2011. I called a great game on a great ship where I met the president and some patriotic guys and gals. These servicemen and women don't have time to waste on social media. Nothing moves them like an actual written or typed letter from home. They wish for nothing more than interpersonal time with their loved ones. They instead spend their time as brothers and sisters in the cause of freedom. **Talk about togetherness! They are a TEAM!** Every minute, they are on-call to protect us and our relationships. Don't take being face-to-face with your friends and family for granted. In our culture, we often talk about athletes being heroes. An athlete is someone to admire and respect in the same way we look up to entertainers and musicians for what they accomplish with their talents. Genuine heroes are like those people I shared a moment with on the Carrier Ship USS Carl Vinson! I met beautiful men and women who represent our nation with pride and passion. They are the true stars of Veteran's Day. The USS Carl Vinson has 4 1/2 acres of American naval ingenuity inside its hull, but what makes it special are the service members who live on it. They serve everywhere so that we're safe anywhere. *That's Awesome, Baby, with a Capital A!*

Dick with servicemen and women on the U.S.S. Carl Vinson.

I get letters asking me about my heroes—these amazing athletes I've seen dishing the rock or pulling off a fantastic dipsy-do dunk-a-roo*.

I've met some great guys over the years. Some of them, like Shaquille O'Neal, made my TEAM for life. Shaq is mobile, agile, and not fragile; he's a player who has a heart as big as his on-the-court presence. When my friend Dale Brown met Shaq, who was 13, on the army base where Shaq's dad was serving, Dale asked, *"How long you been in the Army, soldier?"*

Years later, I saw the 7'1" unique talent pull a rebound and turn it to points so fast that I went off! It was a fan-

> *From Dickie V's DicKtionary
>
> *Dipsy-do Dunk-a-roo – a "Vitalese" term; a fancy slam dunk.*

tastic, unbelievable, unimaginable, but still achievable play of the moment, of the period, and of the game. I interviewed Shaq after that game. He had just achieved stardom as a scholastic athlete by becoming a prestigious McDonald's High School All-American! When we spoke, I barely stood up to his chest, but he was as nice as could be and I've been friends with that gentle giant ever since. He's big, tough, and physical. As big and successful as he is, though, he is still caring and giving and he gets a greater thrill out of giving than receiving. He never for-got where he came from. Shaq was (and is) a very down-to-earth-person who never let his fame go to his head.

Get your joy from giving.

I'm glad for people like the great Kazaam. **Shaquille O'Neal is a man who understands the importance of**

being a hero in the eyes of young kids. My real heroes, though, would be lucky to stand up to Shaq's knees.

I first met one of these miniature marvels at the *Broken Egg*, the restaurant that serves as my office away from home. The child I met was the blonde-haired, blue-eyed, sweet-as-could-be, little Payton Wright. Along with her parents, Patrick and Holly, she stole my heart. She used to come to the restaurant two to three times per week.

It was out of nowhere that Payton started having pain in her knee. Growing pains are what the doctor thought at first. When a doctor hears about pain in a joint, he checks the joint and if nothing is found, it looks like nothing is wrong, but Payton kept crying. More visits and tests later led to the MRI that confirmed the worst. Her parents will never forget the day the radiologist told them to sit down—he had some bad news. It was cancer. Payton had a tumor in her spine and it was going to metasta-size, meaning it would spread through her body. Patrick and Holly were young, living the American Dream, and they were told that their little girl needed nothing short of a miracle. The Wright family hoped against hope for Payton to be okay. **Time got precious pretty fast.**

I got to know Payton very well. She sat at the front table of the *Broken Egg* and displayed so much courage. The cancer spread to her brain. Payton was paralyzed, in a wheelchair, and she eventually went blind. I watched the life, a young life, an innocent life and a beautiful life, fade from her tiny body. **The joy that family took from the smallest sparks of hope was so inspiring.** A treatment that seemed to be going well or a moment they shared was appreciated. That appreciation is

so much more than the appreciation the rest of us experience every day with our gifts that go way beyond health.

I remember during Payton's courageous fight, I was with my family on a vacation. I was watching my grandkids in the water and on the slides having the time of their lives when my phone rang. It was Payton's father, Patrick calling from *Duke Hospital* where Payton was receiving a long-term treatment.

"This is Patrick, Dick," he said. "I'm so excited. I'm so excited!"

When I asked him what was going on, he cried that it was unbelievable because he got a chance to go to breakfast with Payton. It's the first time she'd been allowed out of the bed. They wheeled her down to the hospital cafeteria and it was the greatest day ever.

Are you serious, I thought? **We take the little things in life for granted.** That moment was golden to him—to share that time with his daughter. I felt total guilt. I felt humiliation. I felt embarrassed that here I was thinking about a flight and the work I had waiting for me while my healthy family was busy enjoying life.

Maximize the day in a positive way and appreciate what you have. That's what the Wright family was doing. That's what they taught me through their TEAM and their togetherness.

Payton fought, but she didn't make it. At the funeral, I was so moved, heartbroken, and touched while I watched her parents do what parents should never have to do. They had to bury their own child.

I told Holly, "We can't bring your little girl back, but we can help others through her." It was the beginning of my million dollar challenge. My family and friends have worked diligently on an annual gala ever since to make sure we meet that fundraising standard to help researchers who are working with kids who are battling cancer. Payton inspired that goal. **What inspires you?**

Every time I get tired because I have to call people, meet with people, pull in favors, and everything else I have to do to make that million dollars happen, I remind myself that this is nothing. This is nothing compared to what those parents go through. This is nothing compared to what Payton went through. Holly helped make a million happen

that first year. She told a room full of the great heroes of the sports world who were gathered to raise money for cancer research that they would always have another chance at a win, another chance to coach another game, but

she would never, ever have another chance to coach her little girl in the game of life.

These people stay on my mind. I don't forget about them. I go to bed thinking about them and their families. You want to know who my heroes are? **If hearts were heights, Payton Wright would have stood eye-to-eye with Shaquille O'Neal.**

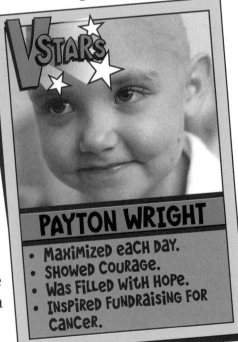

PAYTON WRIGHT

- Maximized each Day.
- Showed Courage.
- Was Filled with Hope.
- Inspired Fundraising for Cancer.

Report
Making **TOGETHERNESS** work for you!

We've been talking about how we build our TEAM, how we expand that TEAM and who we can trust to be on that TEAM. Togetherness is the heart of the T.E.A.M. model for reaching a W in the game of life. Life goals are not about "Me, me!" It's we. *We* grow goals. *We* celebrate the same way *we* achieve, and *we* achieve as a TEAM.

It's not only important to have togetherness to help you reach your goals. It's important because **without a TEAM in your life, achieving your goals won't mean a thing.** I've written books, acted in television and movies, had an amazing career, and seen the best games in the best sport played

"We celebrate the same way we achieve and we achieve as a TEAM."

out live from the best seat in the house. None of it means a thing without my wife, Lorraine (who has been the foundation of my home), my kids, my grandkids, my friends, the great colleagues I have in my ESPN family, and my folks whose black and white picture next to my bible I still look at every day. I operate under the belief that I never want to do anything that would break the hearts of these people... my starting lineup.

It's time to think about your own TEAM. You probably thought about a family member, a coach, a teacher, or maybe a friend as you read through the life stories of some of the people on my TEAM. If that person came to mind, chances are they are on your TEAM.

Build your TEAM. Name three people right now who are in your starting lineup. These are the people who hold a doctorate of love specializing in *your life*:

1. _____

2. _____

3. _____

When it comes to togetherness, we talked about our home TEAM and our first court in life, but we also talked about moving, expanding, and recruiting. You want to associate with quality people. You want a TEAM of winners around you. Build a foundation of good people with good values. Build it with people who are positively contagious to be around and who are always looking at the silver lining, not the cloud.

When you think of these things and if you didn't allow yourself to fear rejection, who could you reach out to today to be a part of your TEAM? Think of three.

1. _____

2. _____

3. _____

Through people like Payton, we learned how important it is to maximize our time with the ones we love and the ones who love us.

Is there somebody on one of these lists who could use a personal note, some one-on-one time, or the sharing of something special from your life? Maybe somebody on one of these lists can offer you a step up on your own ladder of success. How will you maximize your time and appreciate your moment with this person?

_____

_____

_____

Whether online or in-person, it is just as important to cut the bad influences from our lives as it is to add the good influences. You don't want people around you who are making bad decisions. If they're making bad decisions and it's out of your control, it's time to get out of there. You know right from wrong—so do your friends. If it's wrong, it's a bad decision. Don't make it more complicated.

Brainstorm ways to address the negative influences in your life.

_____

_____

_____

_____

What piece of criticism have you received in your life that was hard to take?

_____

_____

_____

How could you use this criticism to your advantage—to be your best you?

_____

_____

_____

What T.E.A.M. building action items from TOGETHERNESS will you *take possession* of in your life with *passion and perseverance (the P's in PRIDE)?* See my togetherness playbook at the end of this book section for hints!

_____

_____

_____

_____

Step Right Up!

USING TOGETHERNESS TO BUILD YOUR LADDER OF SUCCESS

This playbook isn't just about the people we all have in our lives. It's about getting that W—a WIN, in the game of life. It's about **MOTIVATING** yourself through life's obstacles, **ELEVATING** yourself toward your goals, and it's about **BEING GREAT**… greater than you thought you could be. Why all this talk about relationships? **At every step you take toward your goal, you will need people who are willing to help you move up.**

You need to set realistic goals whether you are talking about family, athletics, music and art, or the work world. Realistic goals mean that you need a plan every day, options at every step, and people who can help you achieve those steps.

FROM tHe

M

FiLe

M FOR Motivation!

"If you don't enjoy the climb, how important can the top be?"

~Kenny Rogers

A lot of young people want to jump to the top right away. They don't want to take all the steps in-between that are needed to get to the top. They are impatient and want to get there quickly, instead of experiencing the value of the journey and gaining the knowledge that it provides. Get as much information as possible at every step toward your goal. Some people get frustrated that they aren't moving fast enough toward their dream. **They don't realize that everything done in pursuit of their goals will make them better once they are at the top of their ladders of success.**

Also, remember that it's easy to have a goal and write it down. That's just a goal. What is your commitment? I think of my son-in-law who wanted to be a doctor. He didn't just say, "I want to be a doctor," he thought about the years it would take to get there and the bills he would have to pay along the way. He made a plan to handle each of those steps.

To make the commitment means that you sometimes have to give up something you like for something you love. My daughters were passionate about tennis, and they often had to give up social time to participate in tournaments. What is your plan to get there? **If it's important to you, you'll do the work.** My daughters would often be up a couple of hours before school began so that they could work out and train, looking to gain the winner's edge.

I often share the famous saying: **"Genius is 1% Inspiration and 99% Perspiration."** When you're setting your goals, keep all of these things in mind!

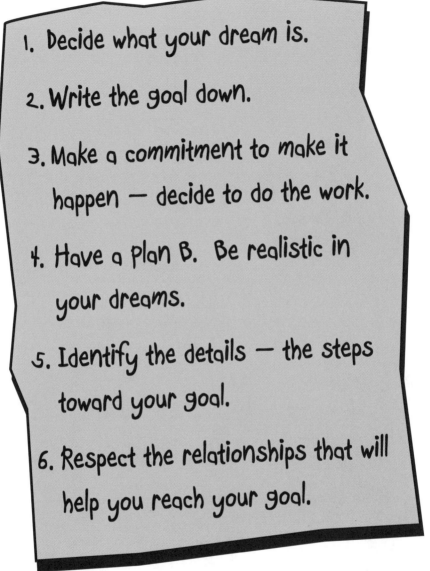

1. Decide what your dream is.

2. Write the goal down.

3. Make a commitment to make it happen — decide to do the work.

4. Have a plan B. Be realistic in your dreams.

5. Identify the details — the steps toward your goal.

6. Respect the relationships that will help you reach your goal.

My success has been no different from any other achievement. I don't just tell you some of the things that will work for getting a W in life. I've lived them.

Chasing my dreams has required making commitments, taking steps, and respecting TEAM relationships. I've used these things to navigate toward my life goals.

MY LADDER OF SUCCESS...

Commitment Card

~~I, Dick Vitale, will coach basketball in college.~~

Plan B

I, _Dick Vitale_, will be a sports broadcaster for ESPN.

Dick Vitale– ESPN's go-to guy in basketball for more than thirty years!

I wouldn't be where I am today, with my ESPN team, without the steps and people who got me here. I still set goals and they all go through the ladder of success.

Dick Vitale– Detroit Pistons Basketball Coach, 1978

Once in the NBA—already surpassing my original goal—I continued to go into every game with research, preparation, and knowledge. It was this commitment that led me to taking on a mentor-style relationship when I began in TV. Jim Simpson took me under his wing and taught me the ins and outs. He reached out to me because I reached out to him. I try to continue his work today.

Dick Vitale – University of Detroit Basketball Coach, 1973

To achieve my goal of college coaching, I first took a job as an assistant coach at Rutgers. I never let an opportunity pass me by. The commitment meant that I had to go to camps and clinics, always gathering as much knowledge as I could about the game that was at the heart of my goal. Relationships were about networking with people at and above my level. Meet people! It's important to ask questions about what you want to do. No question is dumb. Express yourself with honesty and excitement about what you wish to achieve in your life. People love to share and they're willing to share if you open up to them.

Dick Vitale - East Rutherford High School Basketball Coach, 1971

My goal was to be a college basketball coach. The commitment meant that I would have to rack up experience, starting with coaching at the high school level. I continued to apply for jobs all over the country while I also got my Masters Degree to keep working in education—a field I love—if I didn't make it in coaching. My parents were the most important relationship at this level because they believed in me.

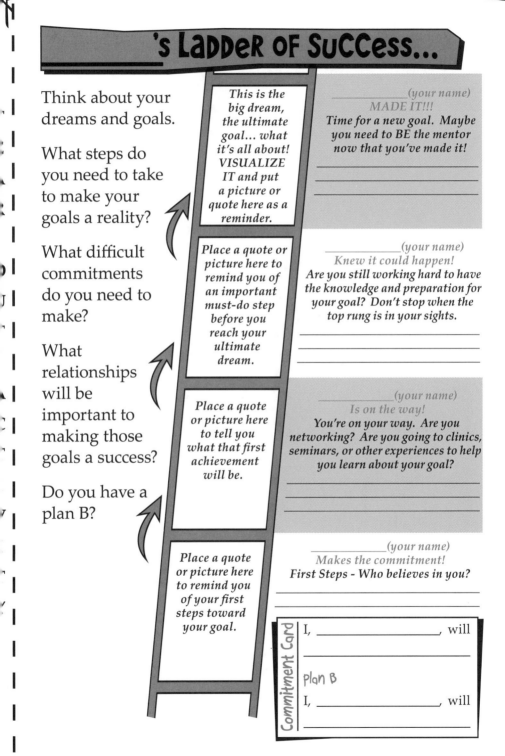

's LADDER OF SUCCESS...

Think about your dreams and goals.

What steps do you need to take to make your goals a reality?

What difficult commitments do you need to make?

What relationships will be important to making those goals a success?

Do you have a plan B?

This is the big dream, the ultimate goal... what it's all about! VISUALIZE IT and put a picture or quote here as a reminder.

Place a quote or picture here to remind you of an important must-do step before you reach your ultimate dream.

Place a quote or picture here to tell you what that first achievement will be.

Place a quote or picture here to remind you of your first steps toward your goal.

_____ (your name)
MADE IT!!!
Time for a new goal. Maybe you need to BE the mentor now that you've made it!
_____
_____
_____

_____ (your name)
Knew it could happen!
Are you still working hard to have the knowledge and preparation for your goal? Don't stop when the top rung is in your sights.
_____
_____
_____

_____ (your name)
Is on the way!
You're on your way. Are you networking? Are you going to clinics, seminars, or other experiences to help you learn about your goal?
_____
_____
_____

_____ (your name)
Makes the commitment!
First Steps - Who believes in you?
_____
_____

Commitment Card

I, _____, will
_____

plan B

I, _____, will
_____

PLACE YOUR LADDER OF SUCCESS WHERE YOU CAN SEE it EVERY DAY.

DiCKie V's TogetHerNess PlAyBook

MOTIVATE by building your team...

Goals are a series of steps, commitments, and relationships.

Persevere against hope.

Without a TEAM, the goals you make lose value.

Everything done in pursuit of a goal will make you better at the goal once you achieve it.

Make a plan to handle the steps of a goal.

Making a commitment means you sometimes have to give up something you like for something you love.

If something is important, do the work for it.

Genius is 1% inspiration and 99% perspiration.

Make new relationships at every stage of your life.

Be inspired by somebody amazing.

Don't fear making the first move.

Stay current with technology.

You are known by what information you put out in the world.

You must study and learn from all that you do in life.

Learn the tools associated with today's technologies.

Friend lists don't always equal friendships.

Don't forget where you came from.

Nobody gets in the Hall of Fame alone.

Do everything with a sense of pride, passion, and work ethic.

Choose your own direction in life.

Thank God for the people who care about you.

Everybody on top got some help getting there.

Do what you love; the money will come.

We all have to grow up.

Have a Plan B.

Continue working to further your knowledge and preparation, even after you achieve your goal.

Visualize your goal.

ELEVATE by building your plan...

Spend one-on-one time with those who care about you.

Share joy with those who bring you joy.

Share special moments with friends to make them feel better-connected to you.

Recognize and remember who is on your TEAM.

Choose your heroes wisely.

Build your starting lineup with quality people.

Don't be around people making bad decisions.

Don't be a recluse; connect.

People love to share and are willing to share if you open up to them.

Reach back to old friends and out to new ones.

Be glad to meet new people.

Stay connected with your first TEAM.

Expand your horizons with a new TEAM.

Learn about the interests of others.

Celebrate loved ones.

Don't ignore those reaching out or reaching back to you.

Find the doctorates of love in your life.

Know when the people in your life are arguing out of love.

Be grateful for those who want to make a better you.

Parents aren't perfect.

True teammates want your best you.

Develop a love for people.

People are people wherever you are.

Don't share something online or in texts that you wouldn't want the world to see.

We aren't complete without connections.

BE GREAT by building yourself...

Nobody wants to be around negativity.

Evaluate criticism to improve yourself.

Focus on the positive.

Don't take blame for other people's relationship choices.

"I love you" is not used enough today.

Recognize love in your relationships.

Love is worth more than material things.

Your place in the world may change, but your personality in it doesn't have to.

Losing touch is a choice... keeping in touch can be, too.

You're changing; so are your friends.

Learn about the people you want to socialize with.

Take joy from hope.

Maximize the day in a positive way.

Don't take the little things for granted.

Extend a hand with love in your heart.

Communicate with letters, emails, phones, and video chatting.

Be yourself in all relationships.

Don't be self-centered.

Don't disconnect from others.

If you don't know a person, he or she probably doesn't know you.

You can't be upset by somebody who doesn't know you.

Take care of the moments in your life.

Nothing makes you feel better than making somebody else feel good.

Recognize how precious time is.

Your heart is your greatest asset.

Show courage.

YOU'RE GONNA BE AWESOME, BABY!

Dick on the job for ESPN with partner Dan Shulman.

Dick hangs with University of Kansas Jayhawks fans.

ENTHUSIASM

From Dickie V's DicKtionary: *When people approach activities with* **enthusiasm***, they uplift those they work with in any phase of life. Their enthusiasm becomes contagious. You have to be your own personality and show enthusiasm in your own way, or you won't enjoy it and it won't be beneficial. You should make an effort to display the three E's... Enthusiasm, Energy, and Excitement for each day. The effort you put into enthusiasm will make the efforts you pour into everything else you do seem that much easier.*

Define... Don't Defend;
Dealing with Rumors and Gossip

You are what you believe...

I believe the things I tell you about passion and pride. I live them. I match my enthusiasm with people half my age and that's the piece of the T.E.A.M. model we need to develop next.

Now that you've got your TEAM, your plan, and your togetherness, you need to focus your mind. **Enthusiasm is a state of mind.** It comes from having something that you are shooting for—something that is important to accomplish. You'll get energized in imagining what that goal looks like once it's been achieved. You have your plan. Put the plan into use and be enthusiastic about it. When you're passionate about something, you're going to have fun and you're going to keep working at it. Sometimes, though, we get distracted from our desire, lose passion for our plan, and let go of our goal.

I remember when I began as an assistant coach at Rutgers University. In a meeting, I asked our coaching staff who we were going to beat with these guys we were recruiting. Lehigh? LaFayette? Columbia? I wanted to beat Kentucky, UCLA and North Carolina!

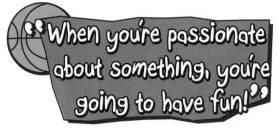

"When you're passionate about something, you're going to have fun!"

They answered, "Get real, man! We're Rutgers."

That was the problem. **If you think you're mediocre, that's all you'll ever be.**

I could see what Rutgers had to offer! It has great academics! It's located in the metropolitan New York area! You mean to tell me we couldn't even find eight blue-chip players? Eight in a four-year period? Two per year? No way, Man. Don't tell me we can't do that! Head Coach, Dick Lloyd, saw it, too. He allowed me to go after the best of the best for our team and it wasn't as difficult as many had envisioned it could be to get them. We recruited some fantastic players, including superstar Mike Dabney and Rutgers' future all-time leading scorer, Phil Sellers.

Those kids we ended up recruiting played a vital role in leading Rutgers to the Final Four in the NCAA Basketball Championship Tournament in 1976.

Those Rutgers players would have a lot to teach to people like Jessica:

> "Everybody talks, especially on Facebook. It's really stressful always having to defend yourself and the truth. You never know what's true about your friends."

What are you doing trying to defend yourself, Jessica? It's no different than when some fans and other critics would laugh when I said I wanted to recruit the best of the best. When people got defensive and started in on the explanation that "We're JUST Rutgers," we had to remind  them what Rutgers was. The mentality of people that our school somehow had less to offer than bigger schools didn't work for us. Rutgers was more than other people's definitions of it. It was a special place. We needed to be enthusiastic, energized, and excited about how to reach a W, rather than letting somebody else define us. Letting somebody else define you is something that never works.

Are you enthusiastic, energized, and excited about what you have to offer to the world?

FROM tHe

M FiLe

M FOR Motivation!

"A man can succeed at almost anything for which he has unlimited enthusiasm."

~Charles M. Schwab

Our class of recruits that year ranked in the top ten of the nation and they were the catalyst to Rutgers becoming a dynamite team. Only you and your TEAM know who you are. With passion, only you and your TEAM know what you can accomplish.

"only you know you!"

With the talent Rutgers had, it could compete with the best and it certainly did under the outstanding leadership of Tom Young, who became head coach after Dick Lloyd. Instead of defending against stereotypes or rumors, Rutgers defined itself as a hard-working and consistent group that epitomized TEAM. The players were unselfish and unified in every manner, and that's why Rutgers was one of America's premier teams.

DeFensive Strategy
Define; Don't Defend

None of what I've accomplished has been through my reputation. It's been through my character and the true person people have come to know.

Along the way in this business and really in anything you do in life, you will always have critics. You can't please everybody and the worst thing you can do is try to make them happy by being somebody other than yourself. I've run across my fair share of articles that have criticized my style and my enthusiastic outbursts.

People may not like my style, my opinions, or my team and player picks, but nobody can ever accuse me of not being prepared, knowledgeable, and excited about doing my job. Remember, those are the things that I *can* control: my preparation, my

effort, and my energy. **I can't control what people say or think.** It's the same way I felt as a teacher and as a coach. What you can control can be seen in all of the broadcasting greats over the years and, honestly, anybody else who has success in any field.

Criticism will come, but I don't need to defend myself against it. **All I have to do is define myself through my actions, my words, and my character.**

Reputation versus character...

So what does it take to develop character and move past the rumors, the gossip, and the negativity that are out there in today's world? The late, great coach John Wooden once shared with me at a public relations seminar we did for a major corporation that reputation was nothing more than what people think about you, but character is developed daily. **Character is who you are.**

One day, while working on this book at the *Broken Egg,* a fellow Tampa Bay Rays baseball fan approached me. He said that he was impressed when he saw me signing autographs and taking pictures with fans who approached me during the game. I was taken aback that he had noticed this because I just thought it was the right thing to do. The only thing that guy had seen

FROM tHe

FiLe

M FOR MOtivatioN!

"Character is something you work on every day of your life."

~John Wooden

was me being myself. **What would people say or think if they observed you just being yourself?** Would you be proud of their opinions? What somebody says about you in-person or online will fade when those who know you or are around you can see your truth.

What another person says about you should be meaningless if you know who you are. You need to act right and make the right decisions. When you do right, you define yourself—you create your character. Instead of defending a critical reputation, you are simply being yourself.

It takes as much energy to have good thoughts, speak good words, take good actions, and create good habits as it does to have negative thoughts, defensive words, bad actions, and poor habits. So choose right! Choose goodness! Choose to be AWESOME! What could anybody say that could possibly stand up against character like that?

When people *know* me, I do care about what they think, but if all they see is my doing right, they can think only of the positive. I didn't sign autographs at a baseball game or talk to people in the stands because I thought I was being watched. **I did it because it was the right thing to do.** It's no different than when Howie Garfinkel saw me praising my East Rutherford High School team. It's no different than when Scotty Connal saw me giving a talk to my University of Detroit team. Your character can become your success. **Reputations from those who don't know you will fade.**

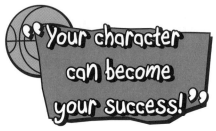

Some young people I know, though, aren't as upset with what is being said *about them* as they are about what is being said or done *for others*.

See what Ben had to say on this matter:

> *"I've been on the soccer team for three years and I just finally made varsity, but there are two freshmen that have made it to the varsity team this year. One of them even plays my position — a position I earned. It doesn't seem fair."*

Ben has a choice. He can choose envy over somebody else's success and achievements, or he can use that example of winning for his own life. What did those freshmen do for that early success? What could be adopted from their training? All  the time people spend worrying about others could be time spent trying to better themselves.

I've told you a lot about one of the greatest coaches of all time, Hall-of-Famer John Wooden, as I've spoken about my TEAM and about enthusiasm. John Wooden was already a major success long before I met him. Did I want to be jealous of that success? Did I want to make excuses for why he became successful? A lot of people do that in the corporate world, in the sports world, in entertainment, in service jobs, in community jobs, and everywhere else in life. **It's easy to make excuses.** It's easy to say people such as Facebook founder Mark Zuckerberg made it because he had Harvard connections or a musician or actor made it because they have a relative in the business. It's easy to say somebody made a team or got a promotion because of an advantage that not everybody had. **Smart people choose instead to learn from the success**—the W—of another person and grab onto the lessons that come with it.

OFFeNSive StRateGY

Appreciate Success

Because there were many people before me who were big-time successes, I was able to make my own map of the greatest path to get there.

When Coach Wooden was alive, I was one of the first recipients of his *Pyramid of Success* award. I was so moved to receive it because it was given in honor of all of the characteristics I so strongly believe in and stand for. The award was based on demonstrating things such as friendship, confidence, and ENTHUSIASM. I was proud to have John Wooden on my TEAM—as an example of success—and see many of those same qualities in him. **I didn't want to envy successful traits. I wanted to emulate them.**

Dick with John Wooden, wife, Lorraine, and daughter, Terri.

Standing Room Only...

I've been really blessed throughout my sports broadcasting career. It's easy for fans to think, *Dickie V is where he is today because of ESPN.* That same ESPN family knows better. **They know that I haven't forgotten where I came from and how I got where I am.** Because of this, they're the ones who took bets out on when I'd begin to get emotional on that night, in 2008, when I was named to The Naismith Basketball Hall of Fame. That was a pretty moving night. This was the biggest honor anybody in basketball could receive and my only wish was that John and Mae Vitale, my mom and dad—people who helped get me there—could have been sitting in the front row at the induction ceremony to see the dream come true.

I held it together. I didn't cry. I just spoke from the heart, so it surprised everybody (even me) when I was overwhelmed at the University of Detroit for a ceremony on December 5, 2011. This time, I was being honored because the school was naming the court after me.   Initially, I

Dick gives acceptance speech at Naismith Basketball Hall of Fame, 2008.

turned them down. I only coached there for five years and didn't feel I deserved an honor of that magnitude. They told me it wasn't just about my years at Detroit, but because of all that I had done for basketball in the more than thirty years since leaving the university. Every time I am introduced on ESPN, it is as the former coach of the University of Detroit Titans. In a commemorative book put out on the occasion, I was called "…college basketball's preeminent ambassador." I accepted the honor.

Dick accepts honors as University of Detroit names its court for him.

I don't know what hit me that night. I was like a water faucet when I saw my old team there and many friends. **Without that place, there is no Dickie V on ESPN.** I don't know where my life would have gone. That place was the beginning of the magic happening in my life. Here was a university that took a young, unproven guy—an assistant from a mid-major college—and made him the head coach of a Division I school. They took a chance on me. They took a chance on the character I could bring to their team. They gave me an opportunity and it was up to me to turn the opportunity into the dream.

When I got the job, nobody thought we would go anywhere. There was a terrific problem of racial divisions in the city and people weren't interested in coming out to our games. I remember calling a team meeting and telling the kids, "My biggest thrill will be when we enter the court for a game one day and there will be a sign on the door that says 'SORRY. SRO' (standing room only). We will become the toast of this city."

People had their doubts, but we went to work to change our reputation into character and our players into the team the city needed. My team, and my first, energetic staff including: Smokey Gaines, Mike Brunker, Jim  Boyce, and Brendon Suhr worked to make SRO a reality. In ensuing years, Smokey, a Harlem Globetrotter's

Hall-of-Famer was Mr. Motor City! He was a loyal, dedicated, tenacious recruiter who was popular in the city. Mike was a spirited, young, go-get-'em assistant dedicated to promoting our program. The three of us worked every corner of Detroit to get the word out.

Are you living your life with low expectations, or are you living in such a way that there is standing room only in the court that holds your TEAM... the court of your life?

Live so that there is standing room only in the court of your life!

Once you bring in the fans, how are you playing at the game of life? **Are you visualizing your goal?** Whatever your goal is, are you imagining what it would be like to achieve it? I made the team sit on the floor of the locker room and think about returning there jubilantly two hours later—champs at the end of the game. **Dream it. Feel it. Believe it.** That's what I wanted them to see.

My son-in-law who was a quarterback and played football for Lou Holtz at Notre Dame also used to practice visualizing. It's important! He would imagine that game-winning pass, picture the receiver catching it, and think about what it would look like when his teammate crossed into the end zone. Dream it. Feel it. Believe it.

Do you have a pre-game strategy? Before my team took to the court on big game days, I remember explaining to them what an upset was really all about. I said, "Fellas,

FROM the M FiLe

M FOR Motivation!

"Winners visualize the rewards of success."

~Lou Holtz

I'm going to define for you what an upset is – not just in sports, but in life."

An upset happens when a five-star team of five-star players plays a team with a lot of three-star players in the eyes of the talent gurus. One game in particular was when the Titans were playing Michigan. This was a definite five-star team, while we were three-star players. (As Super Five-Star Garfinkel would say, a five-star player is big-time;

Dick coaches the action during a University of Detroit Titans game.

he can play anywhere in the nation. A three-star player is defined, more or less, as a mid-major college player.) These were just the facts. To create an upset, three-star players, for forty minutes, must play with a great deal of passion, intensity, and emotion. On that given day, during that given game, and in those forty given minutes, they play like five-star players.

When we played that game against
Michigan, their five-star players
didn't play to their ability. They
were playing like a three-star
team. Sometimes, in those last five
minutes of a game, a team will try
to turn it on and it doesn't work. **In
sports, just like in life, you can't
just turn it on like a faucet. You**
have to be doing it—performing well—consistently.
Consistently believe, achieve, and succeed.

I had told my team, "Fellas, tonight we are going to play
like five-star players. You can't always control the scoreboard," I told my players. The scoreboard is controlled
sometimes by speed, talent, and size. **What we could
control was our effort, our energy, and our enthusiasm.**
It takes no ability to dive for a loose ball. It takes no ability to communicate with one another. It takes no ability
to make one extra pass to get a better shot. That doesn't
take talent; it takes heart and heart can win the game.
Upsets are all about heart.

"We will be a team tonight!" I told them. "We'll be together.
We'll have great effort. We'll
have a great attitude. We'll
communicate. We'll be mentally tough and we're going to
shock the nation tonight."

On the night I was inducted into the University of Detroit
Hall of Fame, several of my players asked me to share
what I made them do before we hit the court for that 1973
game. That night against Michigan, I made them stand
in line… every one of them and, one-at-a-time, I had each

member of my team shake my hand, look me in the eye and say, "Coach, I'll give you everything I have tonight. That will lead to an upset."

On that night in 1973, the Detroit Titans had heart, and I had the first major win in my life as a college coach. University of Detroit 70, Michigan 59! It was upset city, Baby!

Dick celebrates a Titans win.

At the end of that game, many other upsets, many other games, and many other SRO basketball courts, it didn't matter what expectations or beliefs followed that mid-major college team into the match-up. It was what the Detroit Titans did on the court that shaped the opinions about them. They gave it their all and they motivated Motor City, Man!

Are you giving life everything you have?

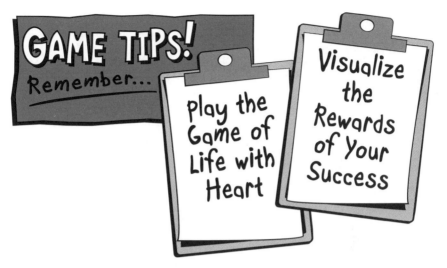

Whether it's rumor mills or gossip mills, reputations or expectations, we are all still in charge of our own truths. Our reputations are ever-changing and our characters are ever-growing. We cancel out the need to defend against negativity when we show our positivity; we move beyond temporary reputations by building our lifelong characters; and we can blow away any expectations those who don't know us have set before us.

We ALL have the ability to be a five star player with enthusiasm!

PTPeR!

Even some of the undoubtedly greatest players have had to face their share of refutation, expectations, and agitation from coaches, players, and even fans. **It's what those players choose to do with that negativity that defines them as a PTPer or a Dow Joneser***. Duke's JJ Redick, now playing in the NBA, was definitely one of the college greats, but he was also one of the greatest at dealing with the abuse a player can take on the road. Redick came strong out of the gates, a Diaper Dandy* from the start, and he kept getting better. It's no wonder opposing teams hated seeing him coming. He was despised, and they were vicious, but it was all left out on the court. **JJ could have taken the abuse and let it drag down his performance, but he chose instead to feed on it and remind them all why he was the guy to beat.** Their defenses would zero in on him and he would zero in on the basket. Redick responded with tenacity to the incredible dislike he endured at away games. He used it as a lift... a lift to National Player of the Year in his senior year; a lift to own the foul line; a lift to the record for most trifectas*; and it lifted him to the status of the ACC*'s numero uno all-time leading scorer!

Redick set a standard, despite disdain from opposing crowds. For responding with nothing but skill, he is the ultimate **PTPer** of *Enthusiasm*!

*From Dickie V's DicKtionary

Dow Joneser – a "Vitalese" term; an inconsistent player; an up and down player.

Diaper Dandy - a "Vitalese" term; a great basketball player who is only a freshman.

Trifecta – a "Vitalese" term; a three-point basket.

ACC – Atlantic Coast Conference of college athletic competitors.

SCHEDULE YOUR SUCCESS; ORGANIZING THE OVERBOOKED
Avoiding the one-dimensional life...

When I do something, I do it 100%. It's how my parents raised me. That enthusiasm is something I never want to face an activity without. It really blew me back when one of my players approached me when I was coaching at East Rutherford High School. He said, "Coach, every time you see me, you never ask about how my life is, how my home is. You only ask about my workout."

He was right. There is a whole list of things that could have been going on that would affect his game. **It's important to get to know the whole person**. Find out what's going on. Make sure the person knows you care about him more than you care about the moment you're in. For me, I was glad that player made me focus on letting him know that I cared.

Balance has always been tough—it's nothing new—but the amount of things to balance seems to grow with every generation.

Straight SHOOTING

Jerome said:

> "We have a lot more to do than our parents and it's really hard to do it all, but we have to. We never get to have a break and we never have time to just vent with our friends. They all have busy schedules, too."

Jerome, it's true that people need to have down time; people need to have balance. When I coached in high school, I was so wrapped up in every detail of my team, my season, my players and the game that there were times my family became something I took for granted. I needed to learn balance. **Balance is important.** You must be multi dimensional.

I learned that I had many parts of my life: faith, family, friends, and my job. You also have to have time to rejuvenate with something that brings you joy or entertainment. If your time is limited, that might just mean that you need to listen to a new song from an artist you like before you go to bed at night. You don't have to have an over-reaching, time-consuming commitment as your form of reenergizing. I like to play tennis and follow music. **These things refresh me so that I am able to have the energy to give all that I need to give to my obligations.** These things—the parts of my life and my hobbies—were all in my personal life circle and I needed to share myself with each of these areas. I was blessed to begin my career in broadcasting, because it helped me find the balance I was seeking. It wasn't my original goal, but it turned out to be the best thing for me. I was able to share my love of the game and my love of family at the same time.

"Share yourself with all aspects of your life."

Sometimes, one area of my life will take more of myself than other parts. When I'm calling games during hoop season, my ESPN career takes a big chunk of my time. When I'm planning my annual gala to raise money for the V Foundation for Cancer Research, my cancer fundraising takes center stage. It's okay for single obligations to occasionally take more of our time as others, as long as all important aspects of your life have a chance to be your number one priority.

DeFeNSiVe StRateGy
Don't be One-Dimensional

Jerome, you need to find an appreciation for the many facets of life you get to experience. Each of those things will add a dimension to who you are becoming and help you to offer more in this world. Read. Educate yourself. Try sports. Appreciate music and the arts. If you need a social break, find ways to build friendships within your activities. The people you're going to want to be around you aren't going to be one-dimensional. **You want to know interesting people, people who have dabbled in all that life has to offer. Why not be one of those people?**

Too many individuals are restricted in their growth. Follow music. Follow news. **Grow culturally.** Spend time reading the headlines so that you can communicate with others. See what's going on in the world so that you can have a conversation. If you're a young man and you're about to go out with a girl who is sports-oriented, it makes you more attractive to that person when you take some time to learn about her passions. Be able to say, "I think the Yankees had a great game yesterday, they're playing really well this year," or "I think the Packers will win the Super Bowl." If it's music, animals, or church that interest her, learn about those things. For a young girl, the same is true. She should learn about the joys of the person she wants to get to know. Spending time in the interests of those you care about is time well-spent. The time you invest in these things is time spent adding to your knowledge and to what you can bring to the relationship and to the world.

Knowledge starts early. My grandkids are all athletically involved. They play tennis, lacrosse, baseball, football, basketball, and anything else that has the word (or the object) "ball" in it. My daughters and their husbands make sure that they also work hard academically. We tell them that they need to have more than just the sports.

FROM tHE
M
FiLe

M FOR MotivatioN!

"The game is evolving. If you're not willing to change and make your game more well-rounded, you're going to find yourself on the outside looking in."

~Chris Dingman

You are working on making a good, whole person. When you reach the age when you're out on your own, you want to have everything possible instilled in you that will lead you to being the very best person you can possibly be.

Whose dream is it, anyway...

There are times when I am so busy trying to balance a little of everything that I wonder how I'll ever get done with anything. My wife, Lorraine, always says to me, "I can't believe all the things you do in the course of the day."

Let's be honest. The real question isn't just about how much should we do in a day. It's about why we choose to do the things we do at all.

According to Will:

> "The worst thing about today is that nobody slows down and we don't even have time to enjoy the things we do. Society's message is work, work, work, but not with any reason for why we work. It seems like it used to be that you worked to get something, but our generation is just supposed to work so that we have more work."

Schedules are so intense today because parents are working hard to help their kids fulfill their dreams. **Activities are introduced**  **to give opportunities.** It's also the job of your parents to prevent the sort of downtime that can be a downfall. Will, I get that everybody needs a break, but not if that break is filled with unproductive things: watching what shouldn't be watched, doing things that shouldn't be done, and seeing sites that shouldn't be seen. **When breaks turn to boredom, bad influences see an opening.**

If there is love, trust, and respect in a home, people do positive things. Trust is built. That building is done on a foundation of responsibilities through activities and those activities should be a foundation for conversation.

Maybe the desire, the dream, the dedication to an opportunity is not shared between you and your parents. **It's your job to find out why you desire, dream, or dedicate your life to that opportunity.** What is the purpose—the end result? You might find out, if you ask, that your parent's goal for your involvement is not what you thought. If you're studying a musical instrument, are your parents looking to advance you musically, or just helping to create a more diversified person? Maybe they just want to introduce you to something outside of your comfort zone. Did you know that music can help you in math, in handling stress, and in growing your confidence? If you're in theater, you learn to work in a group and that's something you'll never escape in this life. Youth groups and churches teach the value of community and helping your fellow man. Hard work in academics mirrors what will be expected of you in college, the military, or a job. Scouting groups teach skills that you carry throughout your life. Sports are a great way to learn about healthy competition—something that you'll need when you are in the working world. **WHY are you doing WHAT you are doing? Ask yourself.**

OFFENSive StRateGy

Discover Purpose

You might not be able to be a top scholar, a first-class athlete or an artist extraordinaire, but could you be a good student who understands the importance of fitness and is capable of enjoying a variety of music? More than likely, that's the sort of person your loved ones are trying to help build. If there are unrealistic expectations related to each of your goals and activities, then that needs to be something you openly discuss with your parents or guardians. **Your loved ones are at the center of your TEAM and communicating with them is a brick in that foundation of love, trust, and respect.**

When I went back to school to earn my Master's Degree in education, I was already coaching and on my way up the ladder toward my goal. This was a time investment. From that investment, though, I grew in my learning about how to work with teams. In that alone, I took joy!

FROM THE M FILE

M FOR Motivation!

"Every choice you make has an end result."

~Zig Ziglar

Think about your activities, especially those you feel are a burden to you. What is it you dislike about, or struggle with, when completing the activities? Now think about them as opportunities. What is a realistic end result for each of those activities? What joy will you get from that result?

Activity	What I Dislike	What's the Purpose?	Where Can I Find Joy?

When you find the purpose in an activity, you find its joy in your life and you can work toward easing its burden.

Take care of today...

You're working toward being your best you. You're learning to find the joy in your activities. You're seeing your schedule as a list of opportunities rather than a list of burdens. This is a start toward the right attitude with your activities, but none of this really causes relief from the stress of getting it all done! You're wondering, *Dickie V, what's the game plan?*

At least, that's what Bella is wondering:

> *"I need serious help with organization! We need to know how to handle it all—even grades. All of our teachers and the books, too, tell us all the things we're supposed to do. We don't have any way of getting them all done, though! How do we schedule it all? When do we do the things we're supposed to do and still have time to do the stuff that's supposed to make us better people?"*

Simplicity, Bella. **Simplicity.** Take care of today. Don't worry about yesterday, because it's gone. Don't worry about tomorrow, because it may not come. Take care of today. **Today is the most important day of your life.**

I always say to have a game plan for the day. Every day, you need to have a plan of what you want to do... what you want to accomplish. You can be your best and do the best you can each day by organizing your time. I think about my wife's appreciation of how much I do. **I can achieve those things because I organize them step-by-step.**

Each day, I know I have to set aside an hour for researching for my job. I spend that time learning about the players and the teams for the game I'll be calling. Sometimes, I have to have an earlier start to my day because I'll be doing an interview before the game. I have specific time set aside for promotional work. I have time set aside for working on my annual cancer research fundraising gala, or for other fundraising for the V Foundation for Cancer Research. I have time set aside to work with the Boys & Girls Clubs of America. I have to take care of my health and fitness. I make time for keeping in touch with my fans. It takes very little effort to write a quick Twitter post if, while I'm researching my work or reading headlines, I see something that could start a good conversation on my feed. The same goes for keeping in touch with loved ones. When I'm on a break while calling a game, I can choose to either waste that time, or pick up the phone and ask how a grandson did in his lacrosse game or how my granddaughter's tennis practice went. You must plan, organize, and manage your time. Make it a priority in your schedule to address what matters most to you.

"You must plan, organize, and manage your time."

Busy is nothing more than a matter of priority. This means that you not only plan for what should fill your time but also you need to get rid of things that are wasting your time. I don't mean downtime… that is effective time needed to refresh, regenerate, and rejuvenate. I'm talking about time spent that is not positive production. **Don't spend time in things that will not help you grow.** That is wasted time! Don't spend time worrying about the achievements of others instead of the lessons of others. Don't spend time with trivial nonsense on the internet instead of reading important headlines and stories that could better and further yourself. Don't spend your entertainment time filling your head with things that only serve to bring you negative images rather than thought-provoking, joy-invoking inspiration and motivation. Spend time in what builds your enthusiasm for life and for the activities you face daily.

Individually, have a couple of things to achieve each day. Mentally and physically, find something positive you want to fulfill each day.

Ask yourself:

What do I have to do today?

_____

_____

_____

Do I need to schedule this day step-by-step?

_____

_____

What is something I can do to grow myself today?

_____

_____

_____

How will I tend to my relationships today?

_____

_____

_____

At the end of the day, see if you achieve what you set out to do. When you accomplish the goals you set for yourself—even the daily goals—it is AWESOME!

GAME TIPS!
Remember...

Take Care of Today

Spend Time on What Grows You

Managing time—using it efficiently, effectively, and enthusiastically—is the key to success.

Dickie Do's and Don'ts!

Do . . .	Don't . . .
Find the reasons for your activities.	Put all of your effort into just one thing or person.
Appreciate your life's many facets.	Feel overwhelmed by your schedule.
Pursue a well-rounded life.	Make assumptions about expectations placed on you.
Share some of yourself with every part of your life.	Waste time in useless pursuits.
Communicate about your involvements.	Worry about past achievements.
Give priority to the people in your life.	Be burdened by what could grow you.
Effectively manage your time.	Give bad influences a good opening.
See your schedule as a list of opportunities.	Forget to take positive down time.

Be a MillioNaiRe of LIFE; Give iN to GiviNg BacK

The price of a great moment...

Talking to young people about putting together their TEAM and following their success models is part of what made me want to join your TEAM through this book. I've spoken to people all over the country who want to hear the stories of successful people and how they became those success stories. **The words shared by so many young ladies and guys are what made me want to provide a guide about how to motivate, elevate, and be great.**

Some people shared that they don't have any time for groups or meetings even though that fellowship with their friends is what helps them to deal with life's adversity. Others shared that they didn't have any people to talk to at all. They hear people say, "Talk to me about anything." But, they also know that this is seldom sincere or that is there is a willingness to listen.

The most difficult thing to hear came from Dhara:

"We get such mixed messages. We're told that we should share, but told that some subjects *are off-limits. Some problems today are just not acceptable to deal with, while others are fine. How do we get the answers we need to the questions that bother us from people who won't judge us?"*

The great news for people like Dhara is this: **There is always somebody who is sincere, genuine, and willing to help.** Sometimes it's up to you to seek that person out, but when you find him or her, you will find the richest hearts and souls you've ever met. **These are the people who have made energy, excitement, and enthusiasm a huge part of their lives.**

I recently spoke with a group at a Boys & Girls Club of America and told them about a young counselor in Sarasota, Florida, who impressed me immensely with his attitude while he helped others. Counselors are not people who are paid the salaries of professional athletes. They don't do it for the money. **They do what they do, not for luxury, but for life and for love.** Talk about enthusiasm! Talk about giving back!

This young man, working hard with today's youth, told me, "Dickie V, I'm a millionaire in LIFE!"

He told me he felt like a million bucks every time he heard about one of "his kids" going to college, getting a career, getting an education, and doing well in life. "To see them do well," he said, "there is no price on that great moment."

That hit home with me. He was dealing with tough kids in tough situations that need all the love and guidance they can get and he felt like a million bucks for it! You

FROM the M FiLE

M FOR MOtivatiON!

"The truth of the human experience is that selflessness is the greatest act you can do for yourself."

~David McCullough, Jr.

don't have to have a million dollars to be a millionaire. **Be a millionaire in your mindset, your attitude, and your actions.** Making a real difference creates real value. That's part of being a good person. My friend, the counselor, is a millionaire because of all the good he does.

OFFeNSive StRateGY

Doing Real Good Has Real Value

Never forget that you are not alone. If you need some-body to recharge your enthusiasm, refresh your energy, or rejuvenate your excitement for life, seek that person out in your home, in your school, in your activities, or in your local organizations. The value that you could find in somebody who wants to be in your life and help make your life good is something that is worth more than mil-lions… it's priceless, Baby!

It's the little things...

Priceless memories and lessons come in all shapes and sizes. More than anything else in life, the courageous kids I've met through the V Foundation for Cancer Research—who are fighting cancer—have taught me about perseverance. They have taught me about chasing the dream, praying without a prayer, and hoping against hope, oftentimes, that they will one day be okay.

Life is full of so much beauty.

Jessica put it so simply:

> *"I guess joy is really just about when you focus on the positive stuff."*

I couldn't agree more, Jessica, but I am amazed to see the exuberance found at the depths of these kids' pains and sufferings. **If they can find enthusiasm in the midst of their daily battles for life, then I can certainly find it in life's daily battles.**

One day, I got a letter. We get so many of them from all around the country and we read them all. My wife gave me one letter and said, "You've got to call this one up. This kid is really something special."

I discovered that Johnny Teis had driven up from Orlando to meet me at the *Broken Egg* in Sarasota when he was in Florida. It turned out that I was out of town and we missed each other. His father explained that Johnny was no longer well enough to travel.

Johnny Teis

"He sent you a green band for cancer awareness," the boy's father told me on the phone. "He sent it to ESPN. It has Johnny's name on it. Do you think you could wear the band while Johnny watches the game?"

That's it? This kid was dealing with cancer and his request was so simple. They sent two new bands overnight for me and my partner, because the mail from ESPN to me might not have reached me in time. Before the Wisconsin vs. Ohio State game that night, my partner and I put on the bands, pulled up our sleeves and made sure the cameras were rolling for that brave kid. We dedicated the game to Johnny and said, "This game is for you. It's going to be a great game!"

We stayed in touch during his battle; a battle he lost in the end. That moment—a little thing like wearing a wristband—gave him a moment of joy. **He saw a positive break in the midst of his struggle, and struggles like Johnny Teis's are greater than those most of us will ever face.**

DeFeNsive Strategy
Find Positives in Life's Battles

Johnny had such a great spirit of life. I am reminded every day through the memories of him and so many others that you can always find something to be excited about.

Throw the party...

If you can have energy (despite your difficulties) and excitement (despite your struggles), then you have discovered the real secret to getting it all... to taking home that championship title in enthusiasm!

Lorraine and I grew up in very simple homes. My wife didn't even have her own room growing up! My parents' home was filled with love, but it was modest. **We wake up every day in awe of our American Dream.** The dream is not dead. The American Dream is as alive today as it was for my parents and uncles who saw how hard work and determination could raise a strong family. The American Dream isn't just alive for athletes and stars and musicians. It's alive for anybody who wants to grab it, shape it, and make it their own. **The American Dream is Awesome!**

Every year, my wife and I give out scholarships through the Sarasota Boys & Girls Clubs of America. One year, we had a girl tell us in gratitude, "I have vowed I am going to make something of myself. I'm not going to live a life of bad choices. Trust me. I will make it one day."

That's the moment! **I have been blessed with much, not to hold onto it, but to pass it on!** I have gained so much enthusiasm in return.

M FOR MotivatioN!

"The best way to cheer yourself up is to try to cheer somebody else up."

~Mark Twain

The younger kids from the Sarasota Boys & Girls Clubs of America aren't ready for scholarships. Instead, we hold a Christmas party for the young ones. We don't just have the party to give gifts but also to let other people know how they can help. We have successful people talk to the kids and show them that there are always places and people to turn to during difficulties in life.

My family, with the help of a special visit from Santa

Claus, makes sure each of the kids has a gift to pick out from under the tree. It is so beautiful to see them open their presents with a spirit of true gratefulness in their hearts. **There are people in this world, in this country, and in our own communities who have nothing!** I see people complain who have roofs over their heads, food in their stomachs, and people in their lives. That is not "nothing." We have seen the real nothing. Every year, we have the hope that other individuals and families who have been as blessed as mine has, will open their hearts and homes to the children of organizations like The Boys and Girls Clubs of America.

When you have a lucky life, pass it on, pay it forward, and give it back! No matter how much you give back and you give away, you will always be the one receiving joy in return... joy for doing right.

"When you have a lucky life, pass it on, pay it forward, and give it back!"

During our Christmas party, I tell the kids that I hope every one of them will be a big success. My dream is that if they become accomplished teachers, famous coaches, top-notch doctors, or successful business owners, they will hold similar parties.

GAME TIPS!
Remember...

The American Dream is Alive

Enthusiasm is Your Return on Giving

After one of those Christmas parties, after I'd given the speech telling the guests that I wanted them to be the successes that carried on the tradition of giving back, one kid approached me.

"I want to tell you this," he said. "I'm going to throw the party."

That moment is worth everything we do.

There is nothing you can tell me that will block your overall attitude of energy, excitement, and enthusiasm. In every circumstance, at every stage of your life, in busy times and downtime, you can choose enthusiasm. It is a state of mind. I have seen people who truly have nothing and people who are fighting for everything hold equally tight to that attitude of gratitude and moments of joy worth more than millions.

Dick shares his children's book, Dickie V's ABC's and 123's with patients on "Dickie V Day" at All Children's Hospital in St. Petersburg, Florida.

Photo Courtesy All Children's Hospital

Awesome, Baby with a Capital A!

Let me tell you about my friend, Adrian Littlejohn. "Little" was part of his name, but it never touched his heart, his mind, or the lives of those who knew and loved him. Adrian was only three years old when he came down with a lethargic sleepiness. His parents and doctors checked everything. An ear infection? The flu? Something simple? Anything but a parent's worst nightmare... a cancerous brain tumor. **This kid fought the battle against that nightmare with radiation, with chemo, and with all that his little body had in way of strength and spirit.** One night, I called Adrian's parents, Ivette and Anthony, to check on the progress of his treatments, only to find out the worst. Nothing was left to do. The chemo was done. The battle was over. Adrian passed away a few days later. I've spoken at a lot of events: black-tie affairs, corporate events, games... this was different. Adrian's beautiful parents asked me to speak at their little boy's funeral. That was by far the toughest moment in speaking I ever had to face. It tore my heart out—tore it out— but I learned a great deal from it, too. I told his dad, "Anthony, you cannot bring your child back. You know it. I know it. We know it. What you can do is live a life that would make your child proud." He went back and finished his degree in education so that he could be certified to teach. Now he's teaching, coaching, and doing the right things in pursuit of his enthusiasm and pride. I can't imagine what it must be like for Anthony to lose his child. However, Anthony had a choice. He chose to face the challenge of moving beyond his pain with enthusiasm. He chose to try and be the best teacher and coach that he could possibly be in memory of his son, Adrian. Ivette, meanwhile, has done all that she can to raise awareness about pediatric cancer. Enthusiasm for life is the choice Anthony and Ivette make to honor Adrian. That choice is *Awesome, Baby, with a Capital A!*

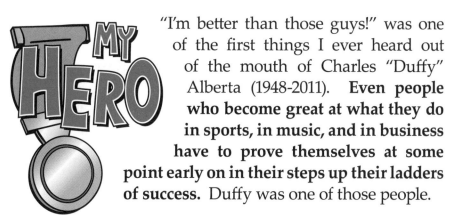

"I'm better than those guys!" was one of the first things I ever heard out of the mouth of Charles "Duffy" Alberta (1948-2011). **Even people who become great at what they do in sports, in music, and in business have to prove themselves at some point early on in their steps up their ladders of success.** Duffy was one of those people.

Duffy was on one of the first teams I coached at East Rutherford High School, but he didn't start out there. When I met the 5'6" tall student, he was shorter than most of his classmates, especially those trying out for the basketball team. He managed to pack a whole lot of spirit into that small body! Something about Duffy made you like him right away.

When Alberta was in high school, I was a new coach in my early twenties. My assistant coach was Bob Stolarz. Bob also coached the junior varsity team. After a tryout, I asked if he thought any of the young guys could help us out on varsity. He pointed to the little guy I'd come to know as Duffy.

Dick working with his East Rutherford High School team.

I said, "Don't even waste my time. No chance. None. Zero. He doesn't have any quickness. Look at his shooting. How's he going to help us?"

Bob told me, "I don't know. There's something about that kid."

I didn't buy it. We posted the team lists that day without Charles Alberta's name. Twenty minutes after the team lists were posted, Bob and I were sitting in our little office when Duffy came in. He was crying, "You cut me! You cut me! I'm better than those guys! You just cut me because of my size. You didn't give me a chance!"

Bob was right. There was something about that kid. You wanted to give him a chance. It took a lot of guts to come into the coaches' office and open up like that! I told him that if he really wanted to be on the team that badly, I'd start him out on junior varsity and he'd have to prove to me I was wrong. **He had to work his way up.**

Duffy knew his strengths. He wasn't much of an athlete or a great shooter, but if I told him to guard somebody, he was on that player like a bug and be in his face all day! More important than his guarding skills, he also turned out to have fantastic leadership ability for the whole team. By the end of the year, Duffy became our varsity team starting point guard, and he helped lead us to the state sectional championship.

One day, Duffy came knocking on my office door looking upset. He said to me after I invited him in, "Coach, I'm really concerned."

When I asked why, he said, "You don't yell at me anymore. You always told us, if I'm yelling at you, it's because I care about you and want your best. I'm getting worried that you don't care anymore." **In addition to knowing his strengths, he always wanted to improve.**

Duffy's enthusiastic, try-hard spirit is part of the reason he went on to run a successful company as an adult. He was very successful in the business world and headed up many high-level board meetings on a regular basis. He ultimately sold the company he had built from the ground up and, never forgetting where he came from, was even able to make a significant donation to the V Foundation for Cancer Research.

Sometimes a hero isn't somebody you immediately recognize, sometimes a hero isn't the fastest performer, and sometimes a hero isn't the person who scores the most points. **Are you missing the heroes in your life?** Are there people in your life who are masters of the skills they know they have? Do they work hard trying to prove and improve themselves?

Charles "Duffy" Alberta wasn't a star player when I first met him, but he became a star team-member for East Rutherford High School and a star in life. For that, he is one of my heroes.

VStars

CHARLES "DUFFY" ALBERTA

- Knew His Strengths.
- Was Tenacious.
- Worked Hard to Prove Self.
- Worked to Improve Self.

Making ENTHUSIASM work for you!

We've been talking about having enthusiasm, about how we keep that feeling in any situation, and about how attacking all of your activities with enthusiasm can help you up your ladder of success. **The enthusiasm part of the T.E.A.M. model doesn't just create a better road toward your goal, it makes you a better person on that road.**

We've also talked about the fact that enthusiasm, like any other characteristic, can be a choice. It's something that should be recognized by you in others; when that happens, people will define you by it rather than by rumors and gossip. If what you put into the world is positive, what people say and think about you will also be positive.

Think about how you have lived your life last week. If somebody who didn't know you observed, what sort of things would they have seen?

Name three positive things that an observer might have seen you doing with your life in the last week:

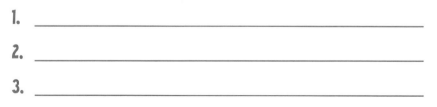

Is there anything negative that an observer might have seen? (Be honest with yourself.)

_____

_____

_____

How could you have better addressed the negative behavior?

_____

_____

_____

Based on your reflections of the last week, how would somebody observing you have defined you? Is this the definition you want? Did you display enthusiasm in your life?

_____

_____

_____

You read about the pre-game strategies of my University of Detroit Titans. Do you take time to visualize your success?

What rewards (personal or material) do you imagine receiving as a result of attaining the goals you set for yourself?

_____

_____

_____

> *In Togetherness, we addressed the importance of setting a plan for your life (your ladder of success). In Enthusiasm, we delved into the details by discussing how important it is to have a plan for each day in order to stay on track for those lifelong goals.*

Take the time to create a detailed schedule for one day and try to live by it. Consider downtime to refresh your spirit, as well as time for each of your activities and the people in your life. Also, reflect on the positive reasons for doing each activity.

StaRt TiMe	END TiMe	ACtivitY	ReasoN FOR DoiNG

Did you feel less overwhelmed after living by a schedule?

Yes   No

I've been lucky in my life to know many giv-ers. I've seen people like Duffy make financial contributions to important causes like the V Foundation for Cancer Research, but—just as important—I've seen people like Boys & Girls Clubs of America counselors give to the people in their lives. Everybody has something to give back and, in return, receive great joy.

What do you have to give back to the world with enthusiasm?

_____

_____

_____

What T.E.A.M.-building action items from ENTHUSIASM will you *take possession* **of in your life with** *energy and excitement (the E's in PRIDE)?* **See my** *enthusiasm* **play-book at the end of this book section for hints!**

_____

_____

_____

_____

Change the Percentage: Using Enthusiasm to Make a Better World

We all need affirmation in our lives. As you work hard to define yourself, rather than defend against negativity, wouldn't it make you feel great if somebody were to say, "Hey! I really like the way you work hard, even though I know you have a lot on your plate!" Maybe you'd love to hear, "Did I ever tell you how much I appreciate you coming to work with a smile?"

We've talked several times about focusing on the positive, and we've talked about how making others feel good is what makes you feel best of all. **Nobody questions that sharing positive moments results in more positive outcomes!** I've mentioned to you that I take the time to drop quick, handwritten notes to those I owe a debt of gratitude or with whom I've shared an important or joy-filled moment.

Even though we know that hearing good things makes us feel good, sharing positivity brings more positivity, and focusing on good things brings happiness, we are failing at doing this as a society! People are quick to jump on sending a letter or email of complaint. **How often, though, do we send a positive letter?** It takes just as little time to say "Thank you!" or "Good job!" as it does to vent about an experience at a store, a restaurant or an event. **The percentage of positive letters sent is miniscule compared to negative rants!**

Imagine how receiving a letter like this could affect a person:

Dear Natalie,

My friends and I came out to lunch at your restaurant the other day. You had a lot of tables and were very busy, but you were nice to me and all of my friends. You introduced yourself, smiled, joked with us, and made sure that our whole order was just right. You checked back and always kept our sodas filled. We were a big group and having somebody do a job with such enthusiasm really added to that day's memory. Thank you so much for doing what you do.

Appreciatively,

Joe

A letter like this, sent to somebody who gave you great service, will lift that person's spirits and keep them working enthusiastically at the job. **Everybody should know that what they do in life makes a difference.**

Think about your daily routine. Is there a teacher, gas station worker, restaurant server, mail or package delivery person or checkout person who was doing a great job? Imagine doing that job yourself. What are the hours like?

Is this person pulling in millions of dollars for taking the time to pack your groceries just right or deliver your mail on time? Are there championship and award ceremonies held for the best server? **Your words are those paychecks, those awards, and those championships.**

Instead of overlooking people in our lives who we take for granted will do jobs to the best of their abilities, take a moment to focus on them. Who are they? What do they do? What about their jobs helps to make your day better?

Person: _____

Job: _____

Positive Observation: _____

_____

_____

Person: _____

Job: _____

Positive Observation: _____

_____

_____

Use the next page to write a letter to somebody at his or her place of employment. **Give a shot of enthusiasm to somebody who needs it!**

Place
Stamp
Here

DiCKie V's ENtHUSiaSM PLaYBOOK
MOTIVATE by having purpose . . .

The effort you put into enthusiasm makes efforts in pursuit of your goal seem easier.

When you're passionate about something, you're going to have fun.

Choose to do the right thing... always.

Smart people choose to learn from and appreciate success.

Don't envy successful traits; emulate them.

Don't forget where you came from or how you got there.

Visualize your goal. Dream it. Feel it. Believe it.

Imagine the rewards for your success.

Upsets are all about heart.

Choose to meet negativity with positive skill.

Be a whole person.

Grow culturally.

Discover purpose in activities.

Communicating with parents is part of the foundation of love, trust and respect.

Every choice you make has a consequence.

Don't make assumptions about expectations placed on you.

Selflessness is the greatest act you can do for yourself.

Be a millionaire in your mindset, your attitude, and your actions.

Priceless memories and lessons come in all shapes and sizes.

Wake up in awe of your American Dream.

Help those who have nothing.

Enthusiasm is your return on giving.

Small moments can be worth everything you do.

All people have to prove themselves early on in their steps up their ladders of success.

Enthusiasm creates a better road toward your goal.

Send letters recognizing positive achievements.

Your positive words can be like paychecks, awards and championships.

Live so that there is standing room only in the court of your life.

Doing good has real value.

ELEVATE by having balance . . .

Be excited, energized, and enthusiastic about what you have to offer to the world.

What you accomplish in your life will be done through action and not reputation.

It's easy to make excuses.

Have a pre-game strategy

Perform well consistently.

Don't feel overwhelmed by your schedule.

You can control your effort, your energy, and your enthusiasm.

Give life everything you have; play the Game of Life with heart.

Balance is important.

Don't allow hobbies to overtake your obligations.

Share yourself with all aspects of your life.

Today is the most important day of your life.

You can achieve daily goals by organizing them step-by-step.

Plan, organize, and manage your time.

Don't spend time in things that will not allow you to grow.

If there is joy during daily battles for life, there is joy in life's daily battles.

Have two things to achieve each day.

Don't put all of your effort into just one thing or person.

Don't revel in past achievements.

Give priority to the people in your life.

Don't forget to take positive down time.

Do what you do, not for luxury, but for life and for love.

Life is full of so much beauty.

Find positive breaks in the midst of your struggles.

When you have a lucky life, pass it on, pay it forward, and give it back.

Give life all you have in way of strength and spirit.

Be willing to work your way up.

Keep trying to improve.

Appreciate your life's many facets.

Don't waste time in useless pursuits.

BE GREAT by having character . . .

Enthusiasm is a state of mind.

Only you know you.

Define yourself instead of defending yourself.

You can't control what people say or think.

Define yourself through actions, words, and character.

Character is who you are.

Character is something you work on every day of your life.

What another person says should be meaningless if you know who you are.

Reputations from those who don't know you will fade.

Your character can become your success.

Don't be one-dimensional.

Be an interesting, well-rounded person.

Activities are introduced to give opportunities.

Spend time on what grows you.

Communicate about your involvements.

Don't give bad influences a good opening.

Never forget that you are not alone.

You are blessed, not to hold onto blessings, but to pass them on.

Be tough and tenacious.

Know your strengths.

Don't miss the heroes in your life.

Enthusiasm makes you a better person on the road toward your goal.

Everybody has something to give back.

We all need affirmation in our lives.

Sharing positivity brings more positivity.

Everybody should know that what they do in life makes a difference.

Give a shot of enthusiasm to somebody who needs it.

If you think you're mediocre, all you'll ever be is mediocre.

There always is somebody who is sincere, genuine, and willing to help.

YOU'Re GONNa Be AWeSOMe, BaBY!

Dick with Hall of Fame memorabilia.

Dick spends some time with basketball camp attendees at Cardinal Mooney High School in Sarasota, Florida.

Attitude

From Dickie V's DicKtionary: *Attitude is defined by the taste for success and the desire to attain it despite any obstacle. A positive attitude is refreshing and always has a person seeing the glass half-full rather than half-empty, living life on an optimistic note. If you have a good attitude, then you're able to be successful and bounce back. It means you're open-minded and able to attack issues in a very positive way. If you choose to develop a negative attitude instead of a positive one, then it will take you to the valley. I want you to get to the top of the mountain!*

Be Good to People—They'll be Good to You; Why Respect Matters

My mom was right...

I've already told you that my mom taught me so much about life. She taught me about love, about appreciation, and about how to succeed in the game of life. Some pieces of her advice have stuck with me from the start and never let me down, including this one: **If you're good to people, then people will be good to you.**

It sounds simple because it is. When I tell young people this advice, though, they think I mean be good to the *right* people or be good to *certain* people. That's not the advice that has helped me build relationships all my life. Unfortunately, that is what my mom's words turn into when young people hear them and then act on them through only some relationships. Perhaps, they are being good to their parents but not to their teachers, good to their boss, but not to their server, or good to their friends, but not to a new student. **Being good to people means you should be good to people in your life—all people in your life—no exceptions.**

I had to smile when I heard Jason say:

"I like stories about people that aren't famous, too. Like people I can relate to."

I treat the people in all areas of my life, no matter their circumstances, with the same kindness, civility, and cordiality as I treat a player who I interview after a game, or a great coach. All people serve a purpose and when I send respect out, I get respect back. Everybody I've ever met who has long-lasting success treats  others with dignity and respect. What you put out in the world comes back to you again and again.

The truth is, Jason, whether rich or poor, in a position of power or working up the ladder, famous or not, you can never be certain just who you're talking to or, in my case, who you're riding with. Not too long ago, the great person and actor, Denzel Washington, wrote a book about one hundred people who have been successful in their lives. In his book, he highlighted why he believed they were successful. **He shares a passion with me for following the lives of successful people and then giving back;** he used his book to raise money for the Boys & Girls Clubs of America.

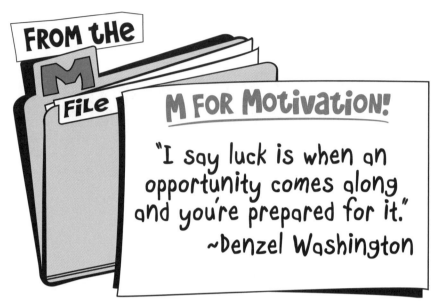

FROM tHe M FiLe

M FOR MotivatioN!

"I say luck is when an opportunity comes along and you're prepared for it."
~Denzel Washington

I was honored to be in those pages alongside Hank Aaron, Willie Mays, and my friend, George Bodenheimer. George is part of my TEAM in the game of life. He's been a part of my TEAM as support *and* as a leader!

When I started at ESPN in 1979, I flew into Bristol, Connecticut, where ESPN began. In the early days of the network, George was the young driver who would pick me up. He would have all of my newspapers for me and I would continue to study on our way to ESPN. George drove, worked in the mailroom, and did filing in the library. He worked his tail off. I remember George saying to me, "Dick, I really want to get in marketing. I went to a great school. Denison. And here I am working in the mailroom."

I would tell him, "George, some day you're going to make it. There's something about you and you're going to make it."

Years ago, I was in the Atlanta airport waiting on a delayed plane. I opened up the *USA Today* sports section and saw the headline: NAMED PRESIDENT OF ESPN—GEORGE BODENHEIMER.

I was so excited for this guy who honestly worked his way up until he landed a fantastic job! President of ESPN? Hey, that's my driver!

I called his assistant and asked to have his voicemail. I couldn't help but have a little fun with

Dick with friend and colleague, George Bodenheimer.

George. On his voicemail, I reminded him of some of those early conversations we had in our rides from the airport to ESPN. "Where am I going? My girlfriend is even mad at me! All I'm doing is working in the mail-room and driving you around, Dick!"

I've worked in the world of sports long enough to know that there are those who are only good to certain people, to "right" people, and to powerful people. How do you know what a person has for his goals? How do you know if a person is busy working hard behind the scenes? **How do you know if the person you talk down to today because he's an assistant, a server, or a driver might not be your boss one day, the person who might play a part in your own goals?** More than these things, how do you know if your positive words and attitude might make a difference in somebody's life? If you're good to all people because it's the right thing to do and not because they can do some-thing right for you, you'll never have to worry about how another person could affect your own journey on your ladder of success and you will have people at all levels pulling for you as you have pulled for them.

OFFeNSive StRateGy
Being Good to All People is Right

When I left George Bodenheimer a message on his first day as president of ESPN, I told him, "George, I don't want a wristwatch, I want a new contract!" **George Bodenheimer is a great example of working diligently and then becoming a giant at what he wanted to do**. He is truly a giant in the world of television. I could joke with him and have his respect because he had mine when he was driving me from the airport and when he was driving forward with his own goals.

Colleagues and accomplishments...

Long before George Bodenheimer was heading up ESPN, I was still new calling a game; and I needed to learn how to operate in the booth instead of on the court. I was lucky to have somebody like NBC's Jim

Dick calling a game with Jim Simpson in the early days of ESPN.

Simpson come aboard at ESPN and help me during my first year, in 1979. Jim Simpson was a megastar, with experience as a sportscaster. It was a big coup for ESPN to sign him during its infancy. Simpson was a major help to me, willing to share his knowledge with me because I asked and because I treated him well. We had respect for one another. Jim took me under his wing; he was a mentor and he taught me how to get in and out of the games I called. **He worked in those areas because I reached out to him with respect and with regard for the position he held and the esteem he had as a great broadcaster.** Jim Simpson taught me the importance of every game and helped me to reach my full potential.

FROM tHe M FiLe

M FOR Motivation!

"Every game you do on that given night is the most important game in the world. Treat it like a championship game."

~Jim Simpson

Jim treated every person and every moment with respect. I gave him the same in return, not just because of his experience, but I respected his work because of the respect *he* gave to his work. **Respect is an attitude based on the understanding of the steps it takes a person to reach a position of status or success.**

Our friend, Jason, continued:

"I get that I'm supposed to listen to my boss at the restaurant, but I'm not going to follow around another server all night. I got paired with a girl who is a year younger than me. It's stupid."

Jason, I never would have learned half of what I did if I decided to judge people by something as superficial as age.

I had more than one talented person to tap into when I arrived at ESPN in 1979. Bob Ley was right there with Jim Simpson from the start. Bob is younger than I, but he gained my respect right away. He gained this sentiment because of his preparation, his knowledge, and his maturity. **There was no shame in reaching out to him for tips on how to be effective because this is a man who was (and still is) effective in his job.**

Bob Ley is an award-winning broadcaster who has shined brilliantly while hosting ESPN's *Outside the Lines*. Why would I want to display an attitude of anything less than respect for what he had accomplished, despite his youth?

Dick with ESPN colleague, Bob Ley.

Don't judge superficial attributes; instead, recognize tangible accomplishments. Respect those who have worked hard to earn the prestige they have attained.

DEFENSIVE STRATEGY
Respect Accomplishments, Not Attributes

It's true I learned a lot from established people like Curt Gowdy, John Wooden, and Jim Simpson, but I've also learned life lessons from children I meet through the Boys & Girls Club of America or the V Foundation for Cancer Research. **I've seen examples of enthusiasm and drive in players of all ages and, even in broadcasting, I've learned from those who were younger than I.** I've learned from people like Bob, who has accomplished a great deal. It is those accomplishments that earned him respect in his industry.

Stranger connections...

I got to know George Bodenheimer well over the years, and I got to work with Jim Simpson and Bob Ley. My mom's words stay with me... her advice to treat those in my life well and treat them with respect. These are all people from different walks of my life who have my love and respect for the roles they play in my life. **You should have an attitude of kindness for those around you and for those with you.** We all have people in our lives, though, who we may barely know at all. Does it really make a difference how we interact with those individuals?

Does Gabby think it matters?

"I just don't have time to email back everybody who helped me on my research project in my class's online forum. Parents don't get it. It's a totally different culture than when they were kids. You don't have to respond to everybody, anymore. That's just not realistic."

Our world has grown smaller, Gabby. We have more people than ever but we can reach across greater distances to connect with them. We communicate with people whose

FROM the M FiLE

M FOR MotivatioN!

"You may delay, but time will not."
~Benjamin Franklin

faces we might not even recognize in person. We have common groups on the internet or in our circles and we don't always feel we owe those connections the time of day. If they've given us the time, though, why would we not offer the same?

In my life, there are times when I am reminded what a difference time can make to these "strangers" of our modern circles. **I try not to procrastinate.** If I delay, all I've really done is added work to another day.

I was calling the Holiday Festival Tournament* in Kansas City. Somebody gave me a note and said, "Dick, this guy's a big fan and his daughter's battling cancer. Could you call him up?" The number was for the Weber family who was supporting their daughter, Lucy.

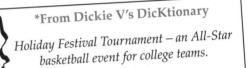

*From Dickie V's DicKtionary

Holiday Festival Tournament – an All-Star basketball event for college teams.

I put the number in my pocket and, to be honest, I forgot about it. I must have been distracted. A while later, the day before Thanksgiving when I was out to dinner with my wife, I had that jacket on and found the note in my coat. I realized, *Oh no. What've I done?* I told my wife that I was supposed to call this family. "Give me 5 minutes," I said.

I called the father and said, "Hey, this is Dick Vitale, Mr. Weber. I just wanted to talk to you for a minute about your little girl Lucy and tell you that they are doing great things with cancer today. I know this because I meet with these doctors."

Her dad was very gracious and thanked me. But he startled me when he said, "Dick, I'm going to her funeral service tonight." It was the only real message that stuck with me. I had no words to tell him for the pain I felt coming through the phone in his voice. I was so sorry and broken up that I didn't call sooner. All I could think about after I returned to dinner with Lorraine was all of the pain the Weber family must have been going through at that time.

I was able to get back to him several weeks later and I told him that we'd love to have his family at our annual gala. They flew out. The V Foundation for Cancer Research was proud to give a research grant in Lucy's name to a hospital. We could help other kids from facing the struggle experienced by Lucy. Do we ever really know what others are going through? Could you make a difference in somebody's life with an attitude of gratitude and grace?

GAME TIPS!
Remember...

You Can't Know a Stranger's Struggles

Kindness is a Gift in Any Circumstance

Nobody expects lengthy letters from those they don't know. It's really not appropriate. Simple notes, emails, texts, or telephone calls, though, take little effort, and they show that you appreciate a person's worth no matter who that person is.

FROM tHe

M

FiLe

M FOR MOTivatiON!

"People don't care how much you know until they know how much you care."
~Joe Theismann

You don't know a person's struggles, goals, or achievements. You don't know if somebody is serving unappreciative people, if he is climbing a ladder of success, or if there is a painful battle in that person's life. If the person is your equal, a leader, somebody who looks up to you, or a stranger in a difficult situation, it doesn't matter. Everybody benefits from kindness. Everybody benefits from mutual human respect. **The person who benefits most of all will be you.**

Mom's attitude—mom's advice—was right. Being good to people comes back to you. People will then be good to you in ways that will change you for the better and  earn you, in return, the kindness, the cordiality, and the civility you project in this world. People will be more willing to support you, to help you, and to join your TEAM for the game of life. **You can't walk down the road toward your W without an attitude of respect toward others.**

PTPeR!

One guy I know, garnering respect as a defensive dynamo, was 2012's Diaper Dandy of the Year, College Player of the Year, crème de la crème, best of the best, Kentucky Wildcat Anthony Davis! The nod for player of the year went to Davis because of his defensive ability; he can change the game instantly with his shot-blocking talent. He may have only been a freshman, but Davis was a flat-out superstar with a powerful game and the leadership skills needed to take the Wildcats straight to the national championship. From there, it was straight to the NBA draft where he was the #1 pick, headed to New Orleans where he will proudly wear his #23 jersey and be a vital part of rebuilding the Hornets program. His teammates were drafted high and will take their games to the pros to compete against the best of the best. Davis earned the respect of his teammates and Coach John Calipari after spending years perfecting the game he played since the age of three. He and his starting lineup showed Kentucky proud outside of the game, too, with a combined 3.12 grade point average. The top players know how to be as good in the classroom as on the court, earning them respect in the game of life as well as in the game of basketball. When Davis landed the Oscar Robertson Player of the Year Award (also for 2012), he easily grabbed the spotlight with all six feet ten inches. He shined that light out to all of those who helped to get him there with an attitude of gratitude and grace. He took to the microphone with thanks for his family, his teammates, and God. He spoke with confidence and humor, displaying loyalty and maturity. If Anthony Davis can face his future with the same passion as he's led his past, he easily wins my respect along with the title of **PTPer of** *Attitude*!

ACCOUNtaBiLitY, ReSPONSiBiLitY, MatURitY; FROM BaD PLaYs to BaD DeCiSiONs

ARM yourselves...

The most difficult concepts to master are respect for yourself, respect for your purpose, and respect for your body. **If you are defining yourself through positive words, actions, and attitudes, you are respecting yourself; if you are building a TEAM of role models and mentors, friends and family, and people with knowledge and preparation to help you reach your goals, you are respecting your purpose.** Respecting your body comes down to making intelligent decisions for your health and against the poisons our world can use to damage your mind, your spirit, and, without a doubt, your body. Intelligence is the "I" in PRIDE!

The best way to make intelligent decisions is to ARM yourself against the wrong choices—the bad choices. **Meet every decision with Accountability, Responsibility, and Maturity!** ARM yourself!

A lot of young people have talent. Talent is nothing but a natural, God-given skill or gift. **What turns a talent into something more, into an attainable goal or dream, is attacking it with desire, dedication, determination, and discipline.** When you drive  forward with these four Ds of life, you have no time for the negativity of excuses, obstacles, or the blame game.

You find out a lot about people, not when they're flying high, but when their backs are against the wall. You find out if somebody is the type of person to drive forward with desire, dedication, determination, and discipline or if he's the kind of guy who would give a list of reasons for why his back is against that wall. **You find out if people are their best after their worst.**

There is a baseball player who I have always had so much respect for and, in five minutes after one game, that feeling for him as an athlete and a person blew straight to the top. That player is Albert Pujols. As a lifetime fan of baseball, meeting him was one of my bucket list* items. I was at the baseball game and was lucky to have great seats near the visiting team dugout. I couldn't wait for the end of the game when I could try to grab Pujols' attention.

Unfortunately, they were beaten... more than beaten. Albert Pujols went 0 for 4 and was in a dramatic slump. After the game, when I made eye contact with Pujols, he smiled and said, "Hi Dick. How are you?" in a very pleasant tone.

*From Dickie V's DicKtionary

Bucket List – a list of goals or activities to do before you die.

I told him simply, "Albert, look. You're going through a tough time, but don't worry. **The cream always rises and you'll be back on top again."**

We were ready to leave him be at that point, but all of a sudden, I heard a voice that said, "Dick, come over here."

It really shocked me as he reached into a bat rack, pulled out a bat, signed it, and said, "I'd like you to have this." My wife and I were thrilled.

What he said next was what point-ed to his character—the character of a star athlete. Here was a guy who had reams of articles written about how he had not yet, at that early point of the season, hit a home run. He could've easily pouted his way down to the clubhouse. He

Dick with Albert Pujols.

could've stomped away. Pujols could have shared, *hey, I'm not familiar with the pitching, yet.* He could have made some other excuse. **A loser blames and makes excuses.** Despite his loss, though, Albert Pujols is a winner in the most important game of all—the game of life. Instead of excuses, obstacles, or blame, he simply said, "I'm not doing what I want to be doing right now… what I need to be doing. But, I know what it is and I will get it done."

My wife and I smiled knowing that Albert Pujols really epitomized what class was about. The scoreboard that night held him Accountable to his performance. He spoke to us about his shortcomings, taking Responsibility for the needs he did not meet. He walked away with a plan to do better, choosing the Mature approach toward preventing a future shut out*; he chose to concentrate on what he could control in the future—his own performance.

*From Dickie V's DicKtionary

Shut Down/Shut Out – a game in which the losing team does not score against the winner.

The decisions we make in response to our defeats are as important as those we make in pursuit of our victories!

OFFENSiVE StRateGY

ARM Yourself When Making Decisions

Albert Pujols has made a lot of decisions throughout his career, decisions that have helped him up his ladder of success and kept him there. **It is his decisions about his attitude, as much as his decisions about his actions that make him an athlete who is accountable, responsible, and mature.** He's a professional with a star attitude and you can count on it that he will be a surefire Hall-of-Famer.

The poison...

If Pujols had chosen to respond to his defeat with negativity, blame, or excuses, I might not have thought as much of him, but he would have another chance to prove himself in another game. He could react differently,  take back his words, and drop his excuses. He didn't have to do any of these things because he is a stand-up athlete. He made good decisions.

Not all decisions can be taken back easily. Some choices can do more than poison the opinions of others. **Some wrong decisions can poison your body, poison your mind, and permanently poison your spirit.**

It breaks my heart when I hear lies like this one from Alyssa:

> *"Everybody either uses pot or drinks. A lot of kids today take their friends' prescription medications, like the A.D.D. drugs and stuff. It helps them get everything done."*

Or Brandon, who added:

> *"(Drugs are) all some people live for and they give up things that they used to like doing."*

The biggest fear parents and loved ones have is their child or children getting involved in the drug and alcohol scene. Brandon and Alyssa should know that it's a complete cop-out when people say, "Everybody's drinking; everybody's smok-
ing marijuana." **It's not true. I don't buy it. I don't believe it... and neither should you.** People who say those things, those false statements, are trying to defend their own bad choices. At the end of the day, the negatives of this lifestyle totally outweigh the positives.

I get very upset when I hear about people doing drugs or drinking heavily because of peer pressure. You want peer pressure? **Follow the people who are doing the right things.** If you want to mess with your heart, though, you're also going to break the hearts of others. That's selfish. You can't prove to me in any way, shape, or form how that is going to make you a better person. There is no victory in it. None. Don't start it.

I've seen first-hand how drugs can create tension in homes, fear and distrust in parents, isolation of drug users, and—ultimately—completely destroy families and lives. Let me tell you about one of the greatest basketball players you've never heard of. My biggest disappointment and one of my biggest personal hurts in my life was Leslie Cason.

Leslie was the golden gift a coach dreams of, a 6'9" high school PHENOM—not just a good player, but a PHENOM—a phenomenal basketball player!

Leslie became a vital part of my team. I'm not where I am today if it were not for Leslie. He gave me my first entrée at the national scene because he was so good that East Rutherford High School had national publicity from the time Leslie was just 14 years old. He was a varsity starter as a freshman, and not just a starter because of his height; he averaged 20 points per game. By Leslie's sophomore year, he was up to 25-30 points per game; in his junior year, he was dominant and led us to two state championships back-to-back. But something was changing. In his senior year, Leslie Cason became very difficult to coach. It broke my heart.

Leslie first came into my life as an elementary school kid who was big and tall, but really was a non-player. I spent hours and hours one-on-one with this kid, separate from even my varsity team. I poured my heart and soul into him. Honestly, I even gave time to him that I should have been giving to other loved ones in my life. He was like a son to me. I loved that kid.

"Leslie, you're not the same kid anymore," I told him when he was a senior. "You're stumbling on the court, fumbling with the ball. We're still winning because of your dominance, but for college, you're going backward. You're messing with drugs, aren't you? I thought you were different."

His response was, "Coach, I thought you trusted me, but you don't. I'm hurt by that. I'm not involved in any drugs." I could tell by his voice, eyes, attitude and body language that he was lying. He was denying the obvious to me and he was in denial of his own dangerous behaviors. He couldn't have looked in  the mirror telling me that lie. He wasn't happy. It showed in his loss of desire to keep being his best.

An element had gotten to Leslie at that time that told him I was using him to get ahead. They said I didn't care about him. I told him he was listening to the wrong people. Where were they when he was unknown? I was there. I was working with him. Where were they when hour after hour I trained with him and helped him become a better player? They're the ones who were new to his life. Not me. **They showed up because of the fame he had... because of who he was. I was there because of how much more I knew he could be.**

Do you have new people in your life who are trying to isolate you from those who have always been a part of your TEAM? **It doesn't matter whether it's an abusive person or an abusive act, the first thing that's necessary for a bad decision to win out is to take away all of the good influence around you.**

I remember telling Leslie that I wasn't planning to go with him to whatever college came calling. I was planning to go coach in college, but I was going to make it on my own. My help wasn't because I needed him to make my goals; it was because I wanted him to make his own goals! **Drugs mess with your reasoning.** He couldn't tell the help from the hurt; he didn't believe me.

The truth is that after his senior year, his grades were so poor that the big schools weren't an option for him. Leslie went to a prominent, national school called San Jacinto Junior College, in Texas. It was a well-known and very popular school for great players who didn't have great grades. This was the go-to college for those players who needed to get their grades up. While in Texas, Leslie kept calling me up, always unhappy. Have you ever had people tell you just how happy they are when they do drugs or are they just looking for the next hit, the next fix, the next poison? **Real achievements can keep you high for a lifetime.** A needle, a puff or a pill fades fast.

By this time, I was at Rutgers and Leslie wanted me to get him into the school. He was still making bad decisions, but he promised me, "Coach, I've changed." **The problem with any kind of addiction, once a person is**

headed too far down its path, is that a person may think he's changed. He may not actually have control over the problem or—more often than not—he's lying to himself and to the world about it. This is true for any addiction—drinking, drugs, pornography, eating binges, video games, gambling, and even unhealthy relationships, you name it. It is vital when battling these addictions to get help from professionals.

I don't know which the case was for Cason, lying or losing, but I wanted to believe in him. I helped him return to New Jersey and become a part of the State University of Rutgers. At that time, I was headed to the University of Detroit as a new coach. At Rutgers, Leslie was nothing more than a marginal player, at best, on a good Rutgers basketball team. He was not nearly as good as he had been or as good as he could have been. **Drugs had robbed too much from him; his dedication, determination, and desire were gone.**

When I made it to the pros as a coach, Leslie wanted me to help him. But, he wasn't the kid with a dream anymore. He wasn't doing the things it takes to be professional. When Leslie was young, the police used to call me up and say, "Tell Leslie to get off the playground." He'd be up all day and night practicing. The lights would be out and he'd still be there dribbling and shooting. People complained about the noise but what I saw was such a beautiful thing.

Leslie was so dedicated. He wanted it. He wanted to be a player. By his senior year, though, he was never out there practicing. You couldn't find him near the court. He didn't care anymore. He was with the wrong people doing the wrong things—partying instead of practicing. He wasn't fooling anybody. This wasn't what it took to be in the NBA.

Leslie didn't last long before drugs claimed him again. Beating drugs isn't a battle you can choose to win once. **For the addict, drugs are a war with battles that wake the user every single day.** Leslie moved away from everybody he knew—his last defense against the poison—because they kept asking him what he was going to do with his life. Again and again, this guy's TEAM tried to reach him. I tried to reach him!

I wonder if he didn't accept help because of opinions like Ashley's:

> *"People don't try to get help because they don't want to be judged."*

All I know for certain is that every hand that reached out to Leslie Cason drove him further away. People weren't judging him; they were trying to help him. **If he had accepted help, the only judgment would have been that he was working hard to defeat the enemy of addiction.**

In 1996, I returned to East Rutherford, the city that was so good to me and played a vital part in launching my career. I was there for the NCAA Final Four* to do studio work on the tournament with ESPN. At that point it was already too late for Cason. He wouldn't even meet with me because he didn't want me to see what he had become.

Early one morning while still in New Jersey, my phone rang. It was a good friend calling to say, "Wait until you see the back page of the New York Daily News. A major story has been done by Ian O'Connor comparing Leslie's journey and the path you took."

*From Dickie V's DicKtionary

Final Four – The games remaining between the last four teams competing in the NCAA elimination-style championship tournament.

I could already see the story in my mind after I hung up: *Coach used player to gain success at the top of the world while leaving kid behind to the drug scene.* I knew how far this was from the truth.

In the story, Leslie could have blamed me or made up lies, but a part of him certainly knew the truth. After meeting with Leslie in the bowery where Cason was peddling drugs, Ian said in the article that ". . . it appeared a simple angle, one man abandoning another, but it happened to be flawed. The coach forever tried to help Cason. The player couldn't help himself."

Leslie told the reporter "Everybody wants me to blame my coach, but there's only one man to blame. The man in the mirror." He was no longer in denial.

I tried to help him again… one more time. I tried to get a hold of him through a community religious leader in his New York neighborhood. I promised all I could possibly do to help him. I made contact with a pastor who was dedicated to helping people in the bowery. I shared my desire to help Les. To get him cleaned up. Get him healthy. Get him off the streets. The pastor was very supportive, but I received a letter from Leslie saying he didn't want me sending money to people in the community because he didn't believe it would ever get to him. Could I send some help, some money, straight to him? I couldn't bring myself to do it, but told him I would give him all that he needed through those local people who wanted to get him through his addiction. **Leslie's thinking had been riddled with drugs and distrust, and he wouldn't take any help.**

In the end, Leslie died of AIDS contracted through dirty drug paraphernalia. He was only 43. Finally, all we could do was sit back and dream of the player he could have been and the man who was never realized all because of drugs. How sad, how tragic, that his life ended like it did.

Because of Leslie's choices and his addiction, he became one of the greatest players who never was and he remains my greatest  hurt and biggest disappointment in coaching. I still feel that it was my responsibility to keep him from a destructive path. It's the same way a parent feels about a child who makes bad choices. He was important to me, and he should today be a retired millionaire in the game of basketball and the game of life. I feel like I lost him. I feel like I failed him.

I had this unbelievably skilled, talented guy, built for the game. To watch what drugs did to him was my

first-hand experience of how drugs and how addiction can destroy individuals, families, and communities. The best decision is to never start down the path of addiction. **If it's too late for that, for God's sake, get help.**

DEFENSIVE STRATEGY
Don't Start Addictive Behaviors

I tried to help Leslie ARM himself. **It's a choice people have to make on their own.** Instead of being Mature enough to recognize the bad influences in his life, he allowed them to lead him off of a successful path toward a career in basketball and onto one toward his demise. Instead of being Responsible for getting himself cleaned up for any one of his many opportunities, he turned away help and turned back to drugs. In the end, he did finally hold himself Accountable, but there wasn't enough of Leslie Cason left to live out his purpose.

Get back up again...

I'm not an expert in the world of drugs and alcohol, but for all my years, I've gotten high on the world, on activities, and on life. A lot of people want to drink and party all night, but I could never understand the thrill of getting high or wasted only to wake up the next day feeling miserable. How is that interesting? How do hangovers equal happiness?

When you're the right drinking age and you want to drink intelligently, there is nothing wrong with that choice. As with any decision, if you are Accountable to the laws that are out there for your health and safety, Responsible in how much you drink and what you do while drinking, and Mature enough to know when it's appropriate and when enough is enough. Alcohol is not in itself a bad thing.

With me, I just didn't ever like the taste. It's not just about right or wrong, it's about how you choose to live. I never drank or smoked just for my peers. If they were going to judge me by whether or not I had a drink with them, they weren't my friends, they weren't people I wanted to be around, and they weren't people I wanted to be with. I didn't mind that my buddies jokingly called me "Mr. Cranberry Juice." I want to be with people who like me for me.

My friend, Danny, nailed it:

> *"Honestly, addictions are really just about community. Some people just do stuff for attention. It's what some groups do together, especially before they can drive and go out and do something. It's all about belonging. It's all about feeling loved."*

Danny, you're right, but love and belonging don't come from addiction of any kind.

One of the most renowned women's tennis players of our day, Jennifer Capriati played the game as a kid with my daughters Terri and Sherri. She blew them away at the young age of 11; she was beating 17 and 18-year-olds like a drum. Capriati made her professional debut at just 13 years old and destroyed a ten-year veteran on the tennis court. She was the youngest player ever to be ranked in the Women's Tennis Association's Top Ten. A couple of years after her big tournament wins began, she struggled. The pressure was too much and instead of turning to her community, she turned to drugs; she was arrested a few times. Then, she took a break from tennis. **Nothing is more important than cleaning yourself up if you are struggling with an addiction or a compulsion. Get Help.** Everything else needs to be on hold until you get yourself together and get back to your best you. You *can* beat addiction with your TEAM.

Capriati was able to clean herself up when she took her break with the support of those who loved her on and off the court… her TEAM. She made the Accountable, Responsible,  Mature choice to get healthy. When she came back, she won fourteen major tournaments, but every day she has to bring her "A-Game" to beat her toughest opponents— drinking and drugs.

If beating addictions is about love, community, and belonging, then the best way to avoid negative addictions is to stay connected to the people who make up the community you belong to and the activities you love—your TEAM. The involvement of my daughters in a lot of activities kept them very busy. They sometimes had to give up what their friends were doing socially, but their positive passions kept them away from many negative influences as well. The communities they belonged to were filled with love, belonging, and people who wanted them to earn a W in the game of life! **If conquering addiction is about love, community, and belonging, why would you do something selfish... something that could hurt yourself and hurt others?**

Jennifer Capriati was able to get back to the top of her game, in tennis and in life, only after she found belonging and community away from her addictions. Then, she reconnected with her love of tennis. Jennifer Capriati was inducted into the Tennis Hall of Fame in 2012 for a career that could have ended early and on a bad note if she had not stopped her decline from pulling her the rest of the way down to rock bottom. Recovery from addiction is a great inspiration to remind us that it's never too late to start making good, right, intelligent decisions.

People think that a famous life is a fantasy life. Fame or fortune does not protect you from the fears and evils of life and society. The famous or rich have the same things to deal with as everybody else in society. Everybody needs something to hang onto to get through the tough times. You can choose to latch onto drinking or drugs, fame or fortune or negative influences, or you can choose to latch onto your TEAM. Latch onto things that will help you make it when you aren't strong enough to make it on your own. Latch onto community, belonging, and love. **Latch onto people who are smart, successful, and striving for a W.**

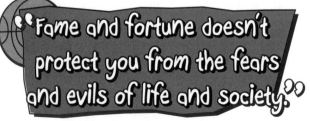
"Fame and fortune doesn't protect you from the fears and evils of life and society."

If you need a hero to latch onto, don't just be enamored with the skills of athletes; look at who they are as people. Look at who they are when they're not competing. Look to people like New York Yankee, Derek Jeter. He's under the microscope in a city like New York. He's smart enough to make good decisions in his personal life, in his relationships, in his attitude. There's no way, for over twenty years, he'd be able to avoid the daily battles if his choices were bad. He does well because he had a good foundation. He knew right from wrong from the start. He's armed with a great TEAM and ARMed for good decision-making.

GAME TIPS!
Remember...

Community is About Love and Belonging

Latch onto Life's Real Highs

You're going to make a lot of decisions in your life and not all of them will have life or death consequences, but all of them will have life consequences. Just as you can take steps upward and forward toward your goal on your ladder of success, you also can slip backward down a ladder of destruction. It happens all the time in our society. You see the headlines coming out about the entertainment industry. Young people, talented people, people with fame, fortune, and opportunity, ending up in trouble. One bad decision leads to another leads to another.

Sometimes it's the kid who started out with *just* pot or *just* pills but ends up losing everything to much more dangerous drugs. What then? **Who gets hurt along the way?** Many times it's not just the victims; it's the criminal. The criminal gives up on life's good chances with every one of life's bad choices.

Every decision you make has the power to move you forward or backward. Never forget that you can always choose to move forward. If you hit rock bottom, you can decide to start your climb back up the mountaintop. It doesn't matter whether your mistake is related to relationships, to your education, or to your physical, mental, or spiritual health.

Look at our world with the right, positive attitude; our world, our culture, our society, offer so many opportunities, so many healthy highs. Falling into addiction of any kind doesn't lead you anywhere, scraping by on crime only leads backwards, poor relational choices are hard to overcome, and drugs are a weak substitute for life's real highs. Get high in the real world, on real accomplishments, and not under the shadow of addiction.

If you've made a lot of mistakes, with the right TEAM and the right encouragement, you can still choose to move forward. Some holes are harder to climb out of than others if you've built a negative track record. It's tough to overcome that, but it can be overcome! At a young age, beat the scene by not starting it. Don't put yourself in that position.

Dickie Do's and Don'ts!

DO...	DON'T...
Meet every decision with accountability, responsibility, and maturity.	Make excuses when you are defeated.
Attack your talents with desire, dedication, determination, and discipline.	Poison your mind, body, or spirit.
Control your own performance.	Believe lies about "everybody" doing drugs.
Follow those who are doing right.	Selfishly hurt yourself or others.
Get high on *life*.	Isolate from the good influences in your life.
Get help if you need it.	Allow distrust against your own TEAM to build up inside of you.
Latch onto smart, successful people.	Let negative influences lead you off of a positive path.
Look at the world with a positive attitude.	Accept drugs as a substitute for real happiness.

NeveR Believe iN CaN't;
ZeRO CHaNCes ONLY Come FROM ZeRO AtteMPts
More of Mom's words. . .

Admittedly, the difficulties I've had to face in my life weren't those that stem from drugs or addictions. I didn't want to do anything that would let down the relationships in my life. I wanted to follow the principles that my parents taught me. **I wanted to live life with passion, hard work, and intelligent decisions.** I wanted to have pride in myself in order to bring pride to my TEAM, but that's not to say I never had my down moments. I've had times when it's been hard to focus on the positive, define myself, and ignore the negativity.

I was in my early thirties, trying to get into the collegiate coaching scene. I was begging to be an assistant—any position would do. We had won two back-to-back championships at East Rutherford where I coached varsity, but I wanted to face the next challenge. I wanted to be a college coach. My buddies said, "Richie, face reality. You never were a great player. You don't know anybody. You're gonna be all your life teaching sixth grade and coaching high school."

There was nothing wrong with that. I love teaching. I think service people are amazing! Teachers, police officers, firefighters, servicemen and women, farmers, and the hard workers who make positive contributions to society are some of the most underpaid people in the world. We give these people the huge responsibility to provide for and guide our kids and to develop our young people. That is an invaluable load to carry and one that is carried every day by those in these positions of serving society. I was as proud to teach as I am to call games on ESPN.

There is honor in being a part of that second line of leadership in children's lives after their parents, but coaching was my dream. I was following my ladder of success: decide the dream, write the goal, make the commitment, be realistic, identify the details, and respect the relationships. I wanted the dream. I wanted to coach.

When I moved from Michigan to Florida, my wife and I could only laugh when we looked at our inch-thick folder of rejections from schools all over the country. **Nonetheless, it takes a toll on you when you hear negativity day after day**, in form letter after form letter. The truth is that I was feeling so rejected on the day when my mom asked, "Richie, you look so down. That's not you. What's wrong?"

I told her that my friends could be right. Maybe I never would be a coach. That's when I got the second piece of advice from Mom that has stuck with me throughout my life.

"I want you to listen to me, Richie," she said, "don't ever, ever—**never believe in can't!**"

If we don't let people define us, why would we let them choose our failures or successes for us? My mom knew more than anybody that you cannot attain your goals, reach your achievements, and make your dreams come true if you're looking at your commitments under the shadow of "I CAN'T." **She helped me realize that one of the biggest ruinations in life is the fear of failure.** The only way I would have had zero chances of attaining my goal is if I had never attempted to reach it.

DEFENSIVE STRATEGY
Don't Accept Can't as an Excuse

FROM the M FiLe

M FOR MOtivation!

Do you know the following people who were told "You Can't":

- One of the greatest science minds ever, Albert Einstein, performed so poorly in school that a teacher asked him to drop out, telling him he would never amount to anything.

- Famous artist Pablo Picasso could barely read or write at the age of 10 and was considered a hopeless pupil with no future.

- Seven-time Tour De France Cycling Champion, Lance Armstrong, was told he had only a 50% chance of beating Cancer and probably wouldn't compete again.

- Thomas Edison, still one of the world's greatest inventors, was described as 'a dunce', 'addled', and, according to his school headmasters, he 'would never make a success of anything.'

- Actress Julia Roberts was born with speech impediments including a stutter.

- Champion surfer Bethany Hamilton lost her left arm to a shark attack.

- Fred Astaire, arguably history's greatest dancer, was described after his first audition with the words: "Can't act. Slightly balding. Also dances."

One leg, one lung, and one amazing life...

You need an attitude of passion and perseverance in your efforts toward your goals.

Take it from Suri:

> *"Just the fact that we're young means we don't have limits, yet. We can choose what we want to do."*

Suri, I couldn't agree more. My friend, Jothy Rosenberg, has become the king of "Who Says I Can't?" the same phrase he used to title his 2009 book about his life.

At just 16 years old, the very athletic Jothy began to suffer from severe pain in his right leg. He'd had muscle pains before, but this was different. Attack after attack of excruciating pain overtook him. His parents, both doctors, had seen a couple of Jothy's episodes of pain. It would always get better until the day came when he collapsed while playing with his dog. Jothy managed to make his way into his car and drive home, but he couldn't get out of the car. He honked the horn repeatedly until his parents came out. All he could say was, "Same knee. Can't walk."

Cancer was the diagnosis and it was just the beginning for Jothy. Doctors had to amputate his right leg above the knee on the very next day. Imagine being a healthy, athletic high schooler one day and having a cancer diagnosis and loss of a leg the next. He could have given in and given up, but he chose to give life his all.

"Don't give in; don't give up; give life your all."

Jothy Rosenberg treated every obstacle as a challenge, beating the healing times assumed by doctors, and mastering a prosthetic leg in nearly half the time that was expected by experts. He even kept his sense of humor, joking to doctors that they had "finally found a cure for (his) athlete's foot."

Who says "I can't"?

Jothy didn't. Three years later, he was faced with another challenge… another diagnosis. The cancer was back and this time it claimed a lung, and, because of chemotherapy, a lot of his strength. Yet he kept his stubbornness and his spirit. After recovering, Jothy worked hard to continue his athletic pursuits. He learned to swim, ski, and bike. He worked to erase the phrase, 'Jothy's a good athlete *considering* he has only one leg or one lung.' Before long, people stopped using that word, *considering*. Jothy is just plain good. He's great. **He's Awesome, Baby!**

Are you trying to make it toward your goal *considering* your obstacles, or are you just trying to make it toward your goal? What could you do if you removed all of those reasons for not being able to accomplish something in your life? Ignore the excuses and just do what you were made to do. Follow your passion, your pride, and your purpose.

Ignore the Excuses

Jothy Rosenberg has one leg, one lung, and one amazing life. He is married with children and he even has grand-children. He earned a PhD in Computer Science, was on the faculty of Duke University, authored two technical books, and started seven high-tech companies. In athletic accomplishments including sixteen swims from Alcatraz to San Francisco and bike races of nearly 200 miles, Jothy has raised significant thousands for charities. **He never believed in can't, never accepted the excuses, and never tried to merely survive. He has thrived!**

Enjoy the journey...

Thriving is what everybody should try to achieve in life. If we were made to just survive, we wouldn't need relationships at all; we wouldn't need goals. We would be fine with food, water, air, and sleep. Surviving isn't what makes us successful. **An attitude of merely surviving is not what gets you a W in the game of life.** Thriving is what drives us forward. Thriving is what you achieve when you live every part of life. Experience the ups and downs—the trials and triumphs—that fall on your path while journeying up your ladder of success.

I was lucky to see somebody I know thriving in his dream. What a night at Raymond James Stadium in Tampa. My wife and I, along with several friends, went to the *"Brothers of the Sun"* concert featuring Tim McGraw and Kenny Chesney. I have seen Kenny several times in

M FOR Motivation!

"The greatest discovery of any generation is that a human being can alter his life by altering his attitude."

—William James

concert and each time I am blown away by the energy and passion he displays during his concerts. He is a true performer!

Dick with Kenny Chesney.

Over 46,000 people filled the stadium and Chesney electrified the entire crowd. McGraw and Chesney did thirty minutes of songs together at the end of the concert, mesmerizing the crowd. Lorraine and I go to a lot of concerts. Those who put their heart and soul in it have great concerts. Those who are just living off past successes and not putting it all out there every time they put on a show are not as enjoyable. These two performers are tops on that big stage. **This isn't the stage these superstars started on, though.**

Years ago, Kenny Chesney and fellow country per-former Toby Keith were opening acts for John Michael

Montgomery, and that was a step up! Before then, Kenny told me he remembered what it was like when he and Tim McGraw used to play in front of a hot dog stand. Do you think Chesney would have moved from hot dog stand to opening act if he had a bad attitude as a street performer? Do you think he would have moved from opening act to superstar status if he had a bad attitude as a newcomer to the world of country music?

Too often, people want to save their positive attitudes for the top of the ladder, the packed stadiums of their achieved dreams. **The problem is you won't get to the big stage unless you have a great attitude as the opening act.**

I have tremendous respect for Kenny Chesney's generosity and support for the V Foundation for Cancer Research. Every year he gives us a donation to help to one day eliminate that horrible disease. He has a great attitude as a successful musician because he has a great attitude helping him earn his success.

GAME TIPS!
Remember...

Your Attitude Affects Your Achievements

Thrive on Every Step Toward Your Goal

If attitude is about the desire to accomplish something despite any obstacle, then no obstacle should be too great to affect your attitude. Your attitude throughout your climb toward your goal is as much a part of the journey as every other detail in your plan for achieving the dream.

Sometimes a good attitude comes out in how you treat others. Are you respecting the people in your life? Sometimes a positive attitude has to do with how you

approach the important, difficult, and life-changing decisions you have to make. Do you have an attitude of Accountability, Responsibility, and Maturity for every choice you face? Sometimes the right attitude means that you keep persevering toward your goal no matter the obstacle and no matter the levels you must pass to reach your objective, your mission, and your purpose. Are you simply trudging along as somebody who is good enough until you have to be great? Or, are you giving every day of your life everything you have to offer?

No exceptions to your treatment of others. No excuses for your trials in life. No bad choices with your TEAM by your side. Make attitude a part of your TEAM and you'll be on your way to a win!

Awesome, Baby with a Capital A!

Robert Montgomery Knight. Bobby Knight. The General. By any name, he is one of the sport's coaching icons of all time. My buddy, the very talented Dan Shulman, and I called the historic game for ESPN on New Year's Day of 2007 in Lubbock, Texas, when Texas Tech edged by New Mexico in a 70-68 win. This wasn't just any win—this was win number 8-8-0, Baby! 880 Wins! With that win, The General became the winningest coach in Division I men's basketball history. The story doesn't end there. Knight had read about Roger Banister, the first person ever to break a four-minute mile in running, and it inspired him. Why stop at 880 when he could be the first coach to top 900 wins? The goal was set and The General assembled his troops. Before he retired in February of 2008, Bobby Knight had 902 wins as a college coach in his 42-year career! The story doesn't end there. Knight had said after his record-breaking game win in 2007 that he hoped those guys who had played for him at Army, watched the game and told their kids, "I was there when he started." At least one of those former cadets had watched. Mike Krzyzewski played for The General from 1967-1969 serving as captain for the 1968-1969 season. In Knight, he had more than a coach. Krzyzewski had a mentor. After his military service, he joined the world of coaching and became known simply as Coach K. On November 15, 2011, Duke's Blue Devils beat out Tom Izzo's Michigan State Spartans 74-69 at Madison Square Garden in New York City for Coach K's… 903rd win! The first tear-filled hug Krzyzewski found following the capture of the title of winningest coach went to his own coach, Bobby Knight, who couldn't have been more proud. Both men have extraordinary accomplishments and extraordinary support for one another. The attitudes of The General and Coach K exemplify great loyalty and mutual respect and that's *Awesome, Baby, with a Capital A!*

I met the great baseball player Josh Hamilton during his first year playing with the Cincinnati Reds. (He now plays with the Texas Rangers.) When the team was playing in Sarasota, I talked to them about decision making, accountability, and responsibility. I talked to them about what their uniforms mean and how kids look up to them, hoping and praying to one day be ballplayers. **You never know who is looking up to you.** I wanted them to understand how powerful that is. Josh Hamilton is one guy in the room who knew exactly what that responsibility meant and how he hadn't always lived up to it.

When Josh was a kid, he was an amazing athlete who played football, soccer, baseball, and ran track. Eventually he focused on baseball. That was the dream. His parents still have a scrap of paper from Josh's grade school days. **He wrote out a detailed plan on how to make it to the majors. He built his TEAM, made his commitment and did everything right.** He made the cover of *Baseball America* while he was still in high school. This guy was a running, pitching, hitting baseball sensation! His 96 mile an hour fastball earned him the nickname *Hammer*.

Hamilton was picked up in the Major League Draft as the number one player by the Tampa Bay Devil Rays. **He kept setting goals** even as he signed for millions of dollars right out of high school. At that point, Josh saw himself spending three years in the minors, fifteen in the majors, and an induction to the Baseball Hall of Fame five years after that. He was on the fast track and taking off! His second year in the minor leagues, he was in a car accident with his parents. His mother was badly injured and could no longer come to all of his games because of her medical treatments. He was not the same with his mother not in the stands.

Too much money and too much time on his hands led Josh to an ugly scene. Today, Josh will be the first one to tell you that he made some decisions that now make every single day a battle with his demons. Every. Single. Day. **Every day is a challenge.**

Josh's back never felt quite right after the accident. He stopped showing up to practice and games and he wasn't playing his best when he was there on the field. He was only 20 years old. Josh began experimenting with drugs and alcohol. He covered his body in tattoos—many with evil signs and symbols that he didn't even understand.

No matter how hard Josh might have tried, he couldn't hide the dramatic changes that took place when drugs became the center of his life. Tampa Bay management knew something had changed, something wasn't right.

A visit to the team's psychologist led Josh to admit his drug usage. This was the beginning of years of failed drug rehabilitations, failed drug tests, suspensions, and Josh's suspension of reality that he could somehow hold onto his dream of making it as a Major League Baseball player while living a life of addiction. He stopped taking the drug tests altogether.

Hamilton had moved well past experimenting with drugs to smoking crack on a routine basis. He should have died many times over with the amount of drugs he took. Instead, he drove away most of those that loved him and didn't even think about baseball anymore. He had lost 50 pounds, lost the title of top prospect, and became the epitome of rock bottom.

Absent from the life of baseball and dreams, Hamilton was lucky to find an organization called *Winning Inning*, a program that dealt with addiction through the fundamentals of baseball and Christianity. **He cleaned facilities, cleaned the field, and finally cleaned up.** It had been years since Josh pitched a ball when he asked others if he could throw a few. They had no idea that this shabby guy working at *Winning Inning* was the once great "Hammer". He was a washed-up star who had never achieved the goals he wrote in grade school to make it into Major League Baseball. He threw the pitch—95 mph. Josh Hamilton still had it.

Tampa Bay still owned Hamilton's contract. They offered him up for $20,000. That's peanuts to the big leagues! Peanuts! Nobody would take this guy who had once signed for millions. He finally did make his way back into baseball in an exchange called the Rule 5 Draft, and he's stayed clean and sober for years. Today, Hamilton plays for the Texas Rangers and his stats are impressive. **Nobody will ever know just how good he could have been, though.**

Josh Hamilton speaks to people all over the country about his struggles, about battling addiction, and about finding the strength to come back. He tells people, **"Don't play** that game of having to fight demons every day! Don't put yourself in that position. Life is tough enough. Why add an extra burden?" Josh attacked his addiction, looked it in the mirror, and decided to take it on. Yet he does have that burden; he does fight those demons.

I told him how I hated to see the way the Rays let him go. Josh looked my wife and me in the eyes and said, "It wasn't the Ray's fault. It was my fault. I made bad choices, bad decisions, and that's what I have to own up to. That's what I do every day." As ugly as it had to get, Josh finally took responsibility for the life he was living.

Josh Hamilton isn't a hero for how he plays baseball and he's definitely no hero for the path of drugs, drinking, and bad decisions he made, but he's a hero for facing battles that are almost never winnable. **He's a great inspiration that tells us how we can bounce back.** You can go through the worst kind of ugliness and come out clean on the other side if you make the choice to live up to your best. Josh has taken the right road and certainly his TEAM hopes and prays that he stays on this path. It is the path of inspiration to others who are trying to beat addiction. That is the path of a hero.

Photo Courtesy Lauren E. Drummond

JOSH HAMILTON

- FACED HIS ADDICTIONS.
- GOT CLEAN.
- TOOK RESPONSIBILITY.
- FOUND HIMSELF AGAIN.

T.E.A.M. Report
Making ATTITUDE work for you!

Attitude, like togetherness and enthusiasm, is a choice. Attitude is a vital part of the T.E.A.M. model to motivate, elevate and be great. **The right attitude affects how you approach your relationships, your decisions, and your opportunities.**

Think about the people in your life and in your community. Are you treating people with equal respect? With the same respect you desire to have from them?

Name some of the people in different areas of your life and think about how you could address them with kind words or a kind act:

Person	Relationship (Equals, Boss, Service Person, Acquaintance, Other)	A Kindness I Could Show

Was there ever a time when somebody you barely knew or didn't know at all performed a kind act for you? How did it make you feel?

_____

_____

_____

We talked about ARMing yourself to make positive, moral, intelligent decisions. What does this look like in practice?

What is the most difficult decision you are facing right now?

_____

_____

_____

List the excuses and obstacles that you feel are preventing you from making the right decision:

_____   _____

_____   _____

Based on what decision you make, are you willing to live with the outcome... be Accountable to the results of your decision? Think about what some of those results are and be honest with yourself.

_____

_____

Is your decision Responsible? Does it affect others in any negative way?

_____

_____

_____

If you were to look back at this point in life, as a mature adult, would you regret the decision you're making? Would it be a decision your loved ones and your TEAM would be proud you made?

_____

_____

_____

Name five things you love to do!

1. _____

2. _____

3. _____

4. _____

5. _____

My guess is that your list doesn't include giving up dreams, pushing away loved ones, or dying young. What could addiction and drugs steal from your life?

_____

_____

A good attitude will be helpful in leading you up every step of your ladder of success, erasing "can't" from your vocabulary, pushing through obstacles, and appreciating the small audiences that come before your full stadiums.

What *"I can't"* statement do you vow to erase from your life today?

_____

What small task, on the way to your larger goal, do you plan to face with a positive attitude?

_____

What T.E.A.M.-building action items from ATTITUDE will you *take possession* **of in your life with** *intelligence and respect; intelligence is the I in PRIDE and respect is the R.* **See my** *attitude* **playbook at the end of this book section for hints!**

_____

_____

_____

_____

A Smile Works A Million Ways

A positive attitude is directly tied to success and happiness. Along with proper nutrition, rest, fitness, education, and avoiding smoking and drinking, it is part of your physical, mental, and spiritual health.

When you create a moment of joy in the lives of others, it will come back to you. **Come home with cheerfulness.** That cheerfulness will catch on and spread. If something positive happened at school, share that. Bring that news home. Spread that joy and let excitement build around that. Celebrate each other. Create joy by sharing it passionately. People have the tendency to bring home the unhappiness, the frustrations, and the struggles, instead of the joys. When you live in an atmosphere of positive attitude that you help to make, your own joy will increase, as will your physical, mental, and spiritual health.

Dick serves alongside wife, Lorraine, as Grand Marshall of a Memorial Day parade.

FROM the M File

M FOR MOTiVATioN!

"It's not your aptitude that counts in life, it's your attitude."

~Charles Swindoll

Carry this card with you as the power of health and happiness in your hand—your attitude reminder to be passionate, purposeful, and positive!

Tear Out and Keep ✂

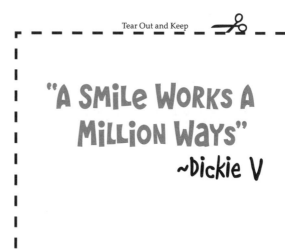

"A SMiLE WORKS A MiLLioN WaYS"

~Dickie V

FROM the M File

M FOR Motivation!

"Being in a good frame of mind helps keep one in the picture of health."

~Anonymous

✂ Tear Out and Keep

- Light up a *room*.
- Light up people.
- Make people want to be together.
- Reach out to others without a word.
- Say hello.
- Be happier and healthier.

DiCKie V's AttituDe PLaYBooK
MOTIVATE by choosing kindness...

If you're good to people, people will be good to you.

Follow the lives of successful people, then give back to secure successes in the future.

Be good to ALL people because it is the right thing to do.

Give respect to those who have earned it.

Respect is an attitude based on the understanding of the steps it takes a person to reach a position of status or success.

There is no shame in reaching out to somebody younger if that person has an admirable skill.

Respect accomplishments, not attributes.

You should have an attitude of kindness for those around you and for those with you.

Kindness is a gift in any circumstance.

You can't know a stranger's struggles.

The person who benefits most from your kindness to others will be you.

You can't walk down the road toward your W without respect for others.

Respect yourself and your purpose.

Find out if people are at their best after their worst.

The first thing that's necessary for a bad decision to win out is to take away all of the good influence around you.

Don't hurt yourself or others with addiction.

Latch onto people who are smart, successful, and striving for a W.

Fame and fortune do not protect you from the fears and evils of life and society.

If you need a hero to latch onto, look at the whole person.

Community is about love and belonging.

There are no winners in a bad decision.

You won't get to the big stage unless you have a great attitude as the opening act.

People look up to you.

The right attitude affects how you approach your relationships, your decisions, and your opportunities.

Come home with cheerfulness.

A smile works a million ways.

Being in a good frame of mind helps keep one in the right picture of health.

It takes a toll on you when you hear negativity day after day.

Dick hangs out with fans before calling games.

ELEVATE by choosing discipline...

Meet every decision with Accountability, Responsibility, and Maturity!

You find out a lot about people when their backs are against the wall.

The cream always rises.

A loser blames and makes excuses.

Decisions about attitudes are as important as decisions about actions.

Some wrong decisions can poison your body, mind, and spirit.

It's not true that "everybody" is doing drugs.

Some people are in your life because of what they know you can become.

Drugs mess with your reasoning.

Once a person is addicted, it's hard to regain control.

Drugs rob determination.

For the addict, drugs are a war with battles that wake the user every single day.

The only judgment on an addict getting help is that he or she is working hard to defeat addiction.

Drugs and addiction can destroy individuals, families, and communities.

Drugs create distrust.

Get help for addictions from those who want your best you.

Don't start addictive behaviors.

Nothing is more important than cleaning yourself up if you are struggling with addiction or compulsion.

You can beat addiction with your TEAM.

The best way to avoid addiction it is to stay connected to the people who make up the community you belong to and the activities you love.

Decisions you make may not always be life or death, but they will always affect your life.

Don't make excuses for defeat.

Don't let negative influences lead you off of a positive path.

Don't accept drugs as a substitute for real happiness.

Every day is a challenge for a recovering addict.

Addicts can never truly hide the changes in who they have become.

Drugs will rob you of knowing just how much you might have achieved.

Have an attitude of accountability in defeat as well as in victory.

BE GREAT by choosing perseverance...

Luck is when you meet an opportunity with preparation.

If you work diligently, you can reach your goal.

Treat every moment like it is the most important.

Don't procrastinate.

Attack your goal with desire, dedication, determination, and discipline.

Follow the people who are doing the right things.

Real achievements can keep you high for a lifetime.

Get high on the world, on activities, and on life.

Control your own performance.

Look at the world with a positive attitude.

Live life with passion, hard work, and intelligent decisions.

Never believe in "can't"!

One of the biggest ruinations in life is the fear of failure.

Don't give in; don't give up; give life your all.

Thriving is what everybody should try to achieve in life.

An attitude of merely surviving is not what gets you a W in the game of life.

Life's journey has ups and downs, trials and triumphs. Appreciate them all.

Your attitude affects your achievements.

Thrive in every step toward your goal.

No obstacle should be too great to affect your attitude.

Your attitude is part of your journey.

Make attitude a part of your TEAM and you'll be on your way to a win!

Write out your plans.

Continue setting new goals.

Life is tough enough without the added burden of addiction.

Anyone who makes positive decisions can bounce back.

A positive attitude is directly tied to success and happiness.

YOU'RE GONNA BE AWESOME, BABY!

Mental Toughness

From Dickie V's DicKtionary: *Mental Toughness* is what winners show in difficult times, when faced with adversity, and when the going is tough. Anyone can feel great when they're getting roses and crowns, but when somebody has bumps in the road—a physical ailment or personal struggle – is when you get to know that person's character. Be resilient. Bounce back to attack the day. Life is not filled with ice cream sundaes with cherries on top; it has ugliness, and it's your job to deal with it with a strong state of mind.

Winner's Edge or Quitter's Edge; Working Hard When the Work is Hard

The coach approach...

Do you know what I love most about that moment just before a couple of really great basketball teams take to the court? As they walk from the locker rooms, their hearts are beating, their nerves are buzzing, and their heads are spinning like a Harlem Globetrotter spins a basketball. In that moment, they're thinking about the training they've put in, their team and their coaches, and the film they've studied. **When you're at the start of your ladder of success, you're feeling some of that same anticipation felt by teams in the pre-game.**

You may be nervous, but what you feel more than anything is excitement. You've used *togetherness* to build your TEAM, you're *enthusiastic* about your possibilities, and you're heading out onto the court with a positive *attitude*.

It's easy to master the first three elements of the T.E.A.M. model when you're at the beginning of your journey. The real test of successful people who want a W—a win in the game of life—is learning how to approach life with that fourth part of the T.E.A.M. model: Mental Toughness.

How do you perform when life gets hard, when the anticipation for your climb has faded and all that remains is the work? Do you want to give up? Mental Toughness is about how, in the middle of life's struggles, you recapture all parts of my success model to motivate, elevate, and be great.

Kelly had something to say about needing to get tough:

"I know I didn't have a good game. I don't really need Dad in my face about it. What good does that do?"

I've seen this many times, Kelly. You have a real educational process on your hands to find a way to communicate with your parents or your coach when you are feeling put down. You also have  to know that they may not be saying it in a way that makes you feel good, but they might still be saying the truth.

Terri and Sherri used to come home after a tournament where they didn't perform well, and they'd feel terrible. My wife, Lorraine, was terrific. No matter how they played—they could have been beaten 6-0—she'd say, "As long as you gave your best today, don't worry about the score. We're going to learn from this situation." Were they any different after losing that tournament than when they won? No. They were still our daughters... total people, not just athletes.

The director of the tennis academy, Nick Bollettieri, the same coach who helped a total of ten #1 tennis players including some you have probably heard of (Andre Agassi, Monica Seles, Jim Courier, and Serena Williams to name a few), had a different approach. Nick would first look for a positive in a performance and *then* offer his critique on areas that needed improvement.

An example would be the following: "I love the way you moved," he'd say to one of them.  "I like how you returned the serve. Your mental approach is outstanding. You're doing great. Now, let's work on your swing or your stance. That will elevate your game to the next level."

Kelly's dad is taking a strict approach; my wife was gentle while acknowledging the poor score, and Nick would compliment but then be firm about what needed fixing. Every one of them, despite their different ways of communicating, is able to notice a common element— sometimes you just need to step up your game.

In the game of life, you won't get to pick what kind of leaders, mentors, or bosses you face. You won't get to pick how they talk to you. You won't get to pick what they ask of you. You need to be mentally tough and respond with that positive attitude regardless of the approach of those around you. Don't let hurt feelings stop you in your tracks before your tracks lead you to the top of your ladder! Winners do not have that luxury. **You need to work hard no matter how you're being asked to do that work.**

DeFeNsive StRateGy
Don't Let Hurt Feelings Stop Progress

If you find yourself crumbling under the pressure because you don't like the way a person speaks to you, you'll never make it in this world. You can use those moments as reminders of how you should choose to communicate with others. That's one way you can process a negative approach. You can also write your thoughts down at the end of the day or choose to defy the negativity by responding with positive performance. Ignoring the sentiment because it's "hard" is not an option. Ideally, everybody in your life and on your TEAM will speak with optimism and encouragement. In reality, you'll hear as many different styles of speaking to you as there are speakers. **You'll be facing far more difficult struggles than words, so learn to deal with those first.**

I want to come home...

My daughters continued in their tennis for years, and I still enjoy playing with them today. Terri eventually ended up with a scholarship to Notre Dame. She had always been an outstanding junior tennis player, and in high school she compiled an outstanding academic record, finishing second in her class. The thing about Notre Dame that was different for her was that most of her classmates experienced the same situation and had similar backgrounds. She was at school for only two weeks when I got a call—Terri never sounded so unhappy.

"Dad, you have no idea how tough this place is academically and in tennis. These kids have 1400 SAT's and a great game!" **She had a major case of a fear of failure—a** *major* **case.**

She was trying to make Mom and Dad happy, proud, and excited, but she feared she wouldn't achieve what we wanted from her.

I gave my daughter two choices. One: I would meet her at the airport and she could quit, but as the saying goes, **a quitter never wins and a winner never quits**. I love her, and if things were tough and she wanted to run, I would have met her at the airport. With the heavy heart of a loving father, I said, "I'm sure there are loads of other places that will love to have you Terri, but when things get tough, you're going to want to run." Then I gave her the other option. Two: I told her to look in the mirror every night and say, "I did everything I could today to be better than I was yesterday as a student and as an athlete." What that meant was to **have a plan**, do a little more studying and to meet with her coach one-on-one when she had no classes. Those extra things are the winner's edge. Do them. If she could do that, she would realize that she was as good as any student there academically or athletically.

Do you want to be known for walking away when life gets tough or for pushing through those obstacles and doing your best? If you plug yourself into every activity you have, be it school, sports, or projects, with everything you have to offer, you will not only do well, you will be refreshed, re-energized, and rejuvenated by the success of your efforts.

OFFeNSIve StRateGY
Develop a Winner's Edge

I was so proud of Terri at her graduation. She received the prestigious *Knute Rockne Award* for her achievements as a student and tennis player, and she followed that by completing her Master's degree as the 2nd highest graduate in her class. At her graduation Terri said to me, "Dad, I never told you this but every day I looked at that mirror and said 'I'm as good as everybody here,' and I believed it."

Fly high...

The key for a lot of people is EXPECTATIONS. We all have individual expectations. Terri assumed that her mother and I held certain expectations and those false beliefs caused her more pressure. **Don't confuse your expectations with the expectations of the world.**

What I control in my expectations when I call a game is to have knowledge through research and preparation. **I have long-term research goals and short-term preparation.** My long-term research is on new players, team histories, and the ever changing rules of the game. My short-term preparation is about knowing the individual teams and players and knowing their strengths and weaknesses. I can control my research and preparation. When I do those things, I am meeting my own expectations. I am confronting my work with a winner's edge just as Terri ultimately confronted her tennis and education with a winner's edge. I can't control whether somebody else out there is also doing well. This is no different from Terri being able to control how the other students at Notre

Dame performed. **What do you expect of yourself?** Don't mix up your ladder of success with the expectations of others. I have to do the best I can at whatever I pursue in life. Terri feels the same way. If you want a W in the game of life, you have to do the same.

If you don't allow yourself to be held back by the expectations of others, you may fly right past those expectations! I was lucky to hear a great speaker talk about the American Dream.

"Don't confuse your expectations with the expectations of others."

General Daniel "Chappie" James, Jr., was the first African American to earn the rank of Four-Star General in the United States Air Force. He was a part of the prestigious Tuskegee Airmen pursuit squadron in the Army Air Corps, later to become the U.S. Air Force and saw action as a pilot in Korea and Vietnam.

When Chappie joined the U.S. Army Air Corps, African Americans weren't yet allowed to fly; the military was still segregated. He came from a tough situation and was the youngest of seventeen kids. His mother taught

young black children in a school where she earned only a nickel a day. People didn't expect much of him as an African American, as a child with so many siblings, or as a pilot in the Army Air Corps.

You think you have a need for Mental Toughness? Here's a guy who grew up in a country that was still racially torn, who was raised in a crowded family, who served in a military that, when he began, didn't provide all opportunities to him, and who spent a lifetime at war fighting for freedoms that weren't allowed to him until many years into his service.

The expectations of our society didn't hold back General James.

FROM tHe M FiLe

M FOR MotivatioN!

"The power of excellence is overwhelming. It is always in demand and nobody cares about its color"

~General Daniel "Chappie" James, Jr.

Chappie flew with one of the greatest units ever to have served in our armed forces and pushed through many barriers to attain the rank of Four-Star General. He blew me away when I heard him speak. He held the same philosophy as John Wooden as he told us to "extend a hand in friendship (to) get love in return." He went on to tell the crowd, "I became something special. There is nothing more special than serving your country. I'm a part of the greatest team of them all—team USA."

GAME TIPS!
Remember...

Have the Knowledge to Meet Your Expectations

Don't Be Limited by Others' Expectations

Terri stopped comparing herself to others and did everything in her power to be the best student athlete she could. Chappie ignored the limitations of his country to become his best... and one of TEAM USA's best. If I feel good when a game ends, I've handled everything I can control. I evaluate myself. If I tell myself that I should have done something differently, then I make sure that I make that change the next time. It's important to have pride in what you do and do it to the best of your ability—every time. The mental discipline to do the things that are in your control is necessary for your success.

Mental toughness begins with the right mental state.

Set expectations. Acquire the knowledge to meet them with discipline. Don't be discouraged from them based on others' critiques, performances, or limitations. Do these things and you will fly fast and high toward your goals.

PTPeR!

Mark Herzlich knew all about flying fast toward his goals. He was an outstanding high school football player who became an All-American college player when he was at Boston College. After his junior year, he was projected to be, by many of the experts including ESPN's Mel Kiper, a top ten NFL draft pick! That's when his leg began to hurt. Despite his trainer's help, the leg never healed. The pain was becoming unbearable. It was time to find answers. Herzlich eventually found his answer in an MRI. The MRI confirmed his deepest fear: it was Ewing's Sarcoma, a rare form of bone cancer. His career was just about to take off and it was stopped in its tracks. He wanted to know what this meant for his future, for his dream, for football! "Forget football," the doctor told him, "I'm hoping we can save your leg so that you can walk." At home, he went to his room and cried for an hour. His parents cried. Then, the mentally tough Mark Herzlich showed his spirit. He walked out of his room to his parents and said, **"Our tears are over now because I'm going to make it.** And, not only am I going to make it, but I'm going to play football again. I don't care what the doctors say."

When Herzlich spoke at my gala for the V Foundation for Cancer Research, he told the crowd that cancer experts may do an amazing job and know cancer, but they don't—in many cases—know the patient. "You don't know me," he said, "because I'm going to play football again." I got to know Mark through the V Foundation gala evening when he was one of our honored guests. **What a well-rounded, special young guy he was.** Herzlich kept his leg, but he lost a lot of his previous strength because of a rod that was now a part of that leg and because of painful, high-risk chemotherapy he underwent as part of his cancer treatment. His draft status was nowhere near where it had been before the Ewing's Sarcoma. In fact, he was not drafted at all. He became a free agent.

I had been so impressed after getting to know Herzlich through the V Foundation for Cancer Research that I spoke to an executive with the Buccaneers; "You need to get this kid! Pick him up as a free agent!" He eventually did sign as a free agent, but not with the Buccaneers; Herzlich became a New York Giant. The team ultimately won a Super Bowl, so Mark stands tall as a Super Bowl winner with the Giants! He busted his gut to prove to all the critics and naysayers that he belonged. Out on that field, Mark wasn't just their token story nor was he

there for pity. He was there because he was good. What an inspiration! You can have adversity, but your will is the battle. Mark Herzlich had an unbreakable will, and for that, he is my *PTPer of Mental Toughness!*

Turning Discipline into Dreams; The Physical Side of Mental Toughness

Sweat's sweet reward...

Too often young people are held back from their best efforts. It's too hot to be outside. It's too cold to have practice. I've got too much to do. We have so many safety measures in place. Sports, in particular, have come so far with technology to protect athletes from everything from dehydration to

FROM the

File

M FOR Motivation!

"Every morning in Africa, an antelope wakes up. It knows it must outrun the fastest lion or it will be killed. Every morning in Africa, a lion wakes up. It knows it must run faster than the slowest antelope or it will starve. It doesn't matter whether you're the lion or the antelope – when the sun comes up, you'd better be running."

~ African proverb

concussions. Nobody wants to be injured or stressed out. If we have proper equipment, water and breaks when it's hot and warm clothes when it's cold, we have nothing but excuses to stop us from hard work.

When did people start thinking that the fruits of labor could be eaten before the labor is spent? When did apathy replace action?

Before ESPN, Detroit, and Rutgers, I coached my East Rutherford high school basketball team. Basketball season is in the winter. We lived in Jersey and it was cold!

I remember one winter practice when it was twenty degrees outside. My team showed up and didn't expect hard work. I told them, "We'll be practicing outside. We will shovel that snow, we will chip that ice, and we will be tough."

On game day we were ready. The other team was coming from a nice, comfortable gym. Our court was nothing different for them. For my team, though, this was luxury.

Parents started out upset and worried. They asked their kids how they felt about the sub-freezing practice. The kids loved it. They had the memory, they were tough, and they had the edge. There are rewards for putting in the extra effort physically. There are rewards for sweat... and they are sweet!

OFFENSIVE STRATEGY

Enjoy the Rewards of Hard Work

When you have a physical edge you aren't afraid to push yourself further. You aren't afraid of a little discomfort because you know the rewards and the rewards are sweeter because of the sweat you shed in earning them. The greatest athletes I've ever known have pushed themselves. They don't take the easy road because that isn't the road that leads to success.

Dad had lessons, too...

Not every person is made to be an athlete. Not every person has a future in physical labor. If that's not the path you plan to take, you still have something to learn from hard work, labor, and physical toughness.

Even Jasmine has something to learn:

> *"I play violin. I'm really good. I've already got scholarships coming. I don't need to know how to lift heavy things or exercise to look good to make it in music. I don't need to work out to be a faster runner either, because I don't even like sports. Those things are a waste of time for me."*

I agree, Jasmine, that having a certain look is not the most important thing to anybody's goal. Labor and fitness, two different things, have results that go far beyond appearance. I never wanted to have the same job as my dad. I had my own dreams and he respected that. I respected my dad for how hard he worked and how dedicated he was to providing for his family.

I observed my dad, John, going to work one summer. He wanted me to see what his job was about. He wanted me to work hard to see what he endured—the sweat shops that he tolerated every single day just to provide for the necessities of life for our family. He always got to work early. Punctuality for him meant that he arrived early. "When the man's paying you," he said, "you have to be there early and ready to work." He also told me that when you're a part of a team, you play by the rules. The rules for his job meant hard work every day. Period. If he hadn't been in there giving his all, there was always somebody else out there who would be willing to take his place. Effort matters.

All day long, my father would press coats. It was physical and it was hot. On the car ride home, I'd understood the lesson. Sweat was pouring down both of our faces and our bodies. "You don't want to do this, Richie," he'd tell me. "Get an education. Go to college."

Dad didn't realize that I was getting schooled from him right then and there in that car. Those days, those hot, sweaty summer experiences were his ways of motivating me to get an education.

Dad didn't realize that I was getting schooled by him when I watched him work.

Hard work provided for a house and family filled with love. Strong work ethic meant that Dad never had to worry about somebody else coming along who would do his job better. Punctuality meant he had respect from his boss, because my dad showed respect. His efforts, every day in that factory, every day in the game of life, earned my respect.

Don't Disrespect Physical Efforts

When you experience physical labor like my school team experienced on an outdoor basketball court in the middle of winter, you have the edge. You develop a discipline for the game of life. My dad had that. It's one of many lessons learned through a job I knew I would never actually hold.

I think of everything my parents taught me, from respect, to mental toughness, to the lessons they thought small—like punctuality, which I think is an incredibly important characteristic respected at every level of your ladder of success—and I realize how blessed I was for their lessons. Even today, everything I do and accomplish is dedicated to the values and principles of John and Mae Vitale, my mom and dad.

The magic formula...

Knowing how my dad worked hard made people want to see him succeed. That's a benefit of labor, physical exertion, and good effort.

Jonathan has a perfect example:

> *"There's one guy on my cross country team that has total natural talent but always complains, eats like crap, doesn't try in practice, and doesn't do any off-season training. Nobody likes him on the team. We're always trying to take him down a notch by beating him on the race course."*

Jonathan, when we see people who are scraping by and don't put in a good effort, it's hard to cheer for them. When you see people who go above and beyond what they need to do for a win, you not only cheer for them, you want to follow their examples, their routines, and their TEAM models for success.

I remember the first time I met the legendary LA Laker Earvin "Magic" Johnson. I wanted to recruit him out of high school for the University of Detroit, so I went up to his home in Lansing, Michigan, before the school day. His mom answered the door and  told us that he wasn't home—he was playing ball. This kid was out on the court shoveling the snow and dribbling the ball as he cleared a path! We're talking about 6:30 in the morning! How many of you would go the extra mile? Do you think he just became magic by accident? It took work; it took education; it took dedication, and it took discipline to make his dream a reality!

Years later, in my acceptance speech at the Naismith Basketball Hall of Fame in 2008, I shared with the crowd the story about how Earvin became Magic. I told the room filled with those who had been instrumental in making basketball into a game that I love about Magic Johnson's days as a high school kid shoveling snow early in the morning so that he could get a workout in before going to school. Magic was rolling in his seat, laughing, and hanging on every word I shared about his early dedication to the sport he would one day own. That dedication led to his having a strong TEAM to help him reach his goals. When somebody shows a willingness to work hard to reach his dreams, support systems are never far away.

Johnson had support from his family of ten; they taught him to be physically, spiritually, and mentally strong. His uncle had him playing games against grown men to help make him tough for the game. His ability to attack his dream didn't go unnoticed by his family, his friends, or even his competition.

The night that Magic was inducted into the Hall of Fame, his longtime rival and eventual friend, former Boston Celtic Larry Bird, introduced him. He talked about telling his brother after a college All-Star game that, in Earvin Johnson, he had just seen the best basketball player he'd ever seen. Over the course of the

Boston Celtic, Larry Bird, goes for the shot over rival player,
LA Laker, Magic Johnson.

two men's careers, both of them pushed the other to play and compete better.

During basketball, Magic Johnson gave his all at every practice and in every game, but in the off-season, his work didn't stop. He would go to the gym every day. He stayed for five or six hours because he knew Larry Bird would be staying for just as long. The  two greats, unwilling to be outdone by the other, kept putting more time, practice, training and effort into the sport they loved.

FROM tHe M FiLe

M FOR Motivation!

"Preparation is the key. Play to win, play hard, and play together."

~Pat Riley

Larry Bird said of Magic, "You made your teammates better, you made your opponents better and you made the game better." Although the famed Celtic and Laker were competitors on different teams—always fighting for the same title—Bird and Johnson became a part of one another's lifetime TEAMs. They brought out the best in each other.

GAME TIPS!
Remember...

Strong Workers Have Strong Supporters

A Winner's Work is Never Done

Unlike Jonathan's teammate, Magic Johnson had the respect of everybody around him. It didn't matter whether it was shoveling outdoor basketball courts as a high school student, practicing hard with his coaches and team as an NBA player, or increasing his training time to match that of his opponents—if there was work to be done, he did it.

When it comes to your goals, do you exert the effort needed to get them done? Do you make good choices about your health and fitness? Do you study? Do you train? Are you the kind of person who quits, makes excuses, or shrugs off potential life lessons? Or, do you have a strong support system because your TEAM recognizes your winner's edge?

A winning edge is having the discipline for the hard work it takes to make your dreams a reality. Discipline is a part of the magic formula… the formula that will help you get a W in the game of life.

What efforts do the winners of dreams similar to yours put forth for:

Health and Nutrition?

_____

_____

_____

Fitness?

_____

_____

_____

Training?

_____

_____

_____

Education?

_____

_____

_____

Other?

_____

_____

_____

Dickie Do's and Don'ts!

Do...	Don't...
Enjoy the rewards of physical effort.	Allow excuses to hold you back from your best.
Give your all—all the time.	Think you can enjoy rewards before you work to earn them.
Be punctual to earn the respect of your leaders and your equals.	Be afraid of a little discomfort.
Get an education.	Expect the easy road to be the road to success.
Earn the support of others through your dedication and discipline.	Ignore the lessons of those who have different life paths than you.
Develop a winner's edge.	Shy away from physical labor.
Match and surpass the efforts of your rivals.	Scrape by on natural ability.
Make good choices about your health and fitness.	Believe in an off-season when it comes to chasing your dream.

Beauty and the Bully; It's All About Self-Esteem

One-eyed guy...

Before a magic formula, snow-covered courts, and lessons from Dad, I had to set my eyes on a goal. Long before setting my eyes on that goal, I lost vision in one eye. I was too young to really remember the injury, but as a child, a pencil to my left eye not only made me forever blind in that eye but also it took away my ability to control the eye's movement. Not having control over my eye used to drive me nuts. It really bothered me.

My parents didn't let me use my one bad eye as an excuse to not set goals or to not do the work that was needed to reach them. They didn't let me feel sorry for myself.

FROM the M File

M FOR Motivation!

"Self-pity is our worst enemy and if we yield to it, we can never do anything wise in this world."

~Helen Keller

"People have worse, Richie," they would tell me. They were right, but dealing with that physical difference also meant that I had to deal with the teasing, the judging, and the bullying that came with it.

In my junior year of high school, it got worse. An infection in the eye was so bad that I had to wear a patch for awhile. I ended up missing most of the school year. Eventually, the eye healed, but now I was a year behind. I still had this eye that couldn't focus and that my classmates recall being infected and covered up. The verbal attacks were relentless at times. I'm no stranger to the kind of bullying that has just started receiving national attention in recent years.

Bella was one of many to talk about this:

How we look, what activities we do, what friends we have, and if we're a good girlfriend or boyfriend are all things that people point to and are so mean about. It's impossible to not get picked on, but it's not always the big things you hear about. Sometimes it's stuff like when a girl is told she's strong, or athletic, or tough, but people never say something nice about how she looks. Those other things aren't meant to be mean, but it starts to make you feel like you don't look good compared to other girls. And that makes you feel like crap about yourself. That's a type of bullying, too, when people judge you to be a certain way because of how you look.

Sometimes I wonder if I could get the job today that I got with ESPN in 1979. **I have succeeded because of my abilities and my efforts, but I was always aware that I didn't look like the other broadcasters.** In high school, some people joked that I was the one-eyed guy. I could laugh that off, but there were times that it really got to me.

It makes me think of Jason's words:

> *We're kind of tired of the word bullying because it's all people talk about, and now you can't even joke around with your friends without a parent or a leader or a teacher thinking you're being a "bully" or "insensitive". We miss being able to joke around with our friends. Sometimes parents are overreacting because it's in the news. I make fun of my friends, but they make fun of me. It's not because we're bullying each other. We're just kidding around. Sometimes, though, people who are joking around with one another cross the line and really hurt feelings.*

I love being able to relax with my friends and tell jokes or kid around. You can usually tell if you're touching on a sensitive subject. Every time a friend has to laugh something off, he might really be hurting inside. I thought I'd overcome any sensitivity about my eye, though. After all, I was succeeding at my dream!

Every time I called a game, I would check with the producers and the assistants to see if they had any notes or critiques for me. **I always wanted to improve.** One night following a broadcast, I was walking down a hall of offices when one of the receptionists stepped into the hall angry. "Dick," she said, "I'm just so mad!"

When I asked her why, she told me that a viewer had called in while I was on the air. "Get that guy off my television screen," he complained. "I can't stand looking at him! I don't know where he's looking. His eye is all over the place. It drives me nuts!"

I was feeling like I was back in school. No matter how well I did my job, I had no control over my eye; I had no control over other people being uncomfortable when they looked at me, and I had no control over whether my appearance would affect my employer. I felt terrible. I know it would have been even harder in today's world. My wife had it right when she said that bullying has always been around, but today it spreads faster and farther than ever before because of the internet.

Ashley would agree with Lorraine:

> *People start things online these days and then bring them into real life. It's easier for people to*

> *hide behind the internet no matter why they're picking on you.*

In social media, things have gotten out of control in terms of bullying, and though it may be true that we deal with bullying from more sides today, one thing hasn't changed. Your TEAM, the right and good people around you, will have your back.

After the incident when a viewer was offended simply by my appearance during a game, I called my boss at the time, Vice President Steve Anderson, and I told him my feelings. I didn't want to hurt ESPN. I understood if they needed to let me go. I asked my boss if I should have surgery to try to correct my wandering eye. Anderson said, "Dick, just be yourself. Do what you think is best for you. It will have no effect on our feelings about you as a broadcaster." **That's when I realized I was part of a family.** The people I worked with knew I cared about my work. They knew I was more than my appearance. They knew I wanted to be the best I could be. They brushed this guy off, and, three decades later, I still call games for ESPN.

You're More than Your Appearance

It wasn't long after this incident that Lorraine brought Terri and Sherri in for an eye-doctor appointment with Dr. Conrad Giles, a pediatric ophthalmologist in Birmingham, Michigan. When he saw the last name, he asked my wife if she was related to ". . . that guy who calls basketball games on TV". He asked my wife if I would be interested in having my wandering eye repaired. Although Dr. Giles didn't usually deal with adults, he said he could make an exception and help take care of my eye. If I was interested I should come in and see him. He was so kind because he didn't want to offend me, but he knew he could help me. I accepted his guidance. It was life-changing for me to have the surgery that fixed my wandering eye.

After the surgery, Dr. Giles said, "I'm going to get rid of those thick, coke-bottle glasses and get you into contacts!" Watch out, Brad Pitt! Here I  come, Hollywood! Conrad Giles and I have stayed in touch over the years, and I owe him so much for taking charge and making this change happen for me.

Because I had a work family who kept me on the air, I was able to be seen by a doctor who eventually found the help I needed to fix my eye. I still can't see from my left eye, but it moves in the same way as a sighted eye. I think there are more good people out there than people like the viewer who called in to complain that the one-eyed guy was driving him nuts.

Bella, I think too many people let their self-esteem be dictated by how they look. You might say, "Man, I look good today. I'm hot. Guys will think I'm pretty." That is so weak. That's just the outside. What about the heart? You can be beautiful in the heart, beautiful in the mindset, and beautiful in what you do in your life.

Be beautiful in your heart, your mindset, and your life.

I've seen similar thinking in some of the sports stars I've met. Some of these athletes have a tendency to judge themselves solely by how they perform. I remember going to tennis tournaments at the Nick Bollettieri Tennis Academy where my daughters trained. Winners would be strutting around on top of the world. Those who didn't make it to the finals or take the tournament would be practically cowering in a corner.

Don't judge yourself by your appearance or athletic abilities. Those are just parts of a person; they're not the whole person. **Many of those who admire an athlete for his skill, an actress for her beauty, or a singer for a great voice, haven't taken the time to look inside themselves to see what they have to offer the world.** You have countless reasons to be proud, and you ignore those reasons when you compare yourself to a different set of gifts than the ones you possess.

Famous actors, athletes, and musicians are in the headlines for problems on a regular basis. They may be gifted entertainers, but do you really want to model them and all of the problems they have? Give me a break! **We need to learn how to be good people.** Respect others, be kind, work hard, and be a total person. **Self-esteem should be dictated by the total person and not by a single gifted area.**

What makes YOU a total person?

_____

_____

Joining the failure club...

You're going to have setbacks in life. You can work hard with your TEAM to make the falls smaller and the bounces back bigger, but nothing great is ever achieved without some difficulty. The higher you climb, the easier it is to slip off of a step and the easier it is to stumble along the journey. A viewer's complaint to ESPN was hardly the first swipe at me on my ladder of success.

The point you need to remember about falling down is that you can't let the fear of failure prevent you from trying at all or from getting back up.

FROM tHe

M FiLe

M FOR MOTiVATiON!

"Think like a queen. A queen is not afraid to fail. Failure is another stepping stone to greatness."

~Oprah Winfrey

You're not going to have success at everything you do. I know. I got fired from the NBA and thought it was the end of the world. That's not a good feeling. Nobody thinks it feels good to go through something like that. It brings you down. I remember the day vividly. It was November 8, 1979. Bill Davidson was the owner of the Detroit Pistons.

He was fair and honest, and I deserved to be fired because I violated everything I believed in. I wasn't living with positivity, enthusiasm, and a winning attitude. All I had done for weeks was complain about us not getting it done and I wasn't changing that fact. It was all negativity about our team's situation instead of positivity and ideas about how to change it.

The Detroit Pistons had finished twelve games; we were 4 and 8. I got called in and I was fired. In 2008, I thanked Bill Davidson in my Hall of Fame speech because that ending became my beginning at ESPN. Who would have ever believed it when he gave me the ziggy*! (How perfect was it that Bill and I were inducted into the Hall of Fame in the same year as contributors to the game we love.)

*From Dickie V's DicKtionary
To be Given the Ziggy – to be fired.*

When Mr. Davidson called me in, all I heard was, "We've decided to make a coaching change." I'll be honest—I cried like a baby. I felt like such a failure. Think about it. All my life, all I'd ever wanted to do was coach. In 1970, I was coaching in high school. By 1978, I was coaching in the NBA. My career exploded. It was like a rocket, man. It took off!

Eight years from high school to the NBA. Then, all of a sudden, it went from way up, in the nosebleeds, in the stratosphere, to rock bottom. Boom. Nothing. My self-esteem was destroyed.

People call me all the time because I like to give to people. I collect an autograph, give a ticket to a game, or maybe hook them up with a free gift. After I was fired, they stopped calling. You know what I found out then? You know who was good to me? My parents. My wife. My TEAM. You find out how vital they are. All those people who I thought were friends were really just associates. I had contacts. I didn't have that many intimate friends.

FROM the M FiLE

M FOR Motivation!

These coaching greats turned failures into successes:

- Tom Landry was 0-11-1 in his first year as head coach of the Dallas Cowboys. He went on to coach in 5 Super Bowls and win 2 of them.

- Chuck Noll was 1-13 in his first season with the Pittsburgh Steelers. He eventually coached his team to 4 Super Bowl Championship wins.

- The inventor of the game I love, Dr. James Naismith was fired after coaching 9 years with the University of Kansas. The Basketball Hall of Fame is named after him and houses the greatest names in the history of the game!

- The University of Kentucky fired its entire football staff in 1959. That didn't hold back future head coaches Blanton Collier of the Cleveland Browns, Howard Schellenberger of the Baltimore Colts, Bill Arnsparger of the New York Giants, John North of the New Orleans Saints, and Don Shula of the Miami Dolphins.

I was embarrassed to go to church on Sunday, even though I couldn't tell you the last time that I missed mass. Faith and family are important to me, but I was depressed. Mass was hard because when I went to church on Sundays, I didn't know the situations of the people around me, but they knew mine. I was paranoid; but I felt like everybody around me was thinking, *that's Dick Vitale. He got fired.*

My wife was responsible for waking me up and getting me out of the funk I was in. Lorraine said, "Hey! You're violating everything you stand for. You got fired. You're not the first. You won't be the last."

It took my daughters' experiences to really snap me back to the pride that I had always tried to live by. The principal of my daughters' school (they were in 2nd and 4th grades at the time) called to explain that my girls were getting teased by the older boys because I had lost my job. He was going to send my girls home.

Terri and Sherri could probably relate to Brandon:

Bullying is not at all like they talk to us about it in classes. It's not like there are individual bullies. It's more of a group effect. It happens in cliques. Whole groups of people gang up on other people who don't believe the same things as them, or dress the same, or

act the same way. Or, sometimes people make fun of
when something embarrassing happens to somebody.

I told my daughters they had better stay in school. **Dad was doing well.**

Failures are just setbacks. Detours. I knew who I was. I knew what I had accomplished in my life. The only way the bullies would have hurt my daughters is if I had let them beat me, if I had failed by giving up on any future success. The biggest bullies I  was facing at that time were my own: paranoia about others' opinions, self-pity, embarrassment, and shame for facing my own routines and TEAM—the things that kept me strong.

If you are traveling to the greatest celebration of your life and you run into a road block, do you stop or do you find another way to get to the party? It's not a dead end. It's just a detour. When Scotty Connal called me up after I was fired from the Pistons, I was ready to get to the party, and I ended up at ESPN for a lifelong celebration of success.

Don't be your biggest bully. The only way any bully ever wins is if you let that group or that person—even if that person is you and the bullying is your own thoughts—force you to give up on the road to your goal and the steps up your ladder of success.

DEFENSIVE STRATEGY
Don't Let Failures Be Dead-Ends

Unfortunately, we do deal with bad communication. We do deal with negativity. **You have to isolate those emotional drains and keep them out of your life.** Bullying, you can't really control. You need to not participate in it and you need to learn to deal with it. Bullies need self-esteem to stop the behavior and you need self-esteem to escape it. **Bullying is weak.** The only way it wins is if the bullied person chooses to give in to the dead end. **Beat bullying back with your strength of mind... your mental toughness.**

Right living and right feeling...

When the setbacks in your life are of your own making and not from a bully, you're still responsible for moving on and moving up. We're guilty in our society of being judgmental. I found out when I got fired that all the people I was talking to about my future job prospects didn't focus on my championships in high school, my time at Rutgers, or my years at the University of Detroit. The questions always included, "What happened with the (NBA's) Detroit Pistons?" I'd sit in an interview for an hour defending my one failure instead of sharing my many successes! It's aggravating, but it's honest—it's reality. If you sit across from an interviewer and you have that mark on your resume, it's hard to overcome.

When that sort of thing happens—when you're judged on your past—it can sometimes feel like bullying. In reality, it's no different than when you need to define yourself against rumors. In time, people will see that you are human and you may make mistakes, but you live your life as well as you can, making good and right choices.

A judge I know often sees court cases where a criminal may start small, by shoplifting. The shoplifter gets braver and takes somebody's purse. This is somebody who is on the way *down* a very negative ladder. Is it going to be grand theft before he stops? It's not an uncommon pattern. Because of that, our society—right or wrong—will often judge a person based on a single wrong action. I've known smart, articulate, hard-working people who are barely scraping by because of a past misdemeanor. Sometimes they are working in the only job that will hire them.

Kelly knows that feelings of shame aren't always obvious:

People don't always see it (bullying) from the outside. They only see the really blatant stuff like pushing people around or some jerk calling people offensive names. Nobody thinks that stuff is okay, but there's so much more to bullying than that. There's more than bullying against specific groups. It's not just against gays, people of other races or religions or nationalities, or non-jocks. Sometimes, it's against somebody who is quiet or old-fashioned, dresses differently or does a lower-class job, or who just doesn't believe the same things that society says we should. Nobody is free from being picked on by some group today, and nobody really notices the stuff that's little, but those are the things that really build up.

If you make a mistake, you need to learn that there is forgiveness in doing positive work. Some of the same people who are in difficult jobs because of a bad mark on their resumes wouldn't trade that work for anything because it is good work, positive work, and work that makes them know they are doing right. After all, our nation is represented by the blue collar trades, like those that my parents and uncles worked in to provide for their families.

Kelly, these are people who have things building up in them, too. They probably felt a little bullied by society and by the judging that people do when they discover past mistakes or even past crimes. **Just like I made my daughters stay in school to keep the bullies from winning, it's important for anybody with a mark on his past to pick up his pride and get back to work, no matter what that work is.** In time, people will see a hard-worker who is moving past bad choices by making new, good choices.

People make mistakes in life. All people. You can't go back from all mistakes, but you can go forward from most of them. Sometimes people want success, but are so filled with guilt that they don't let it happen. They believe the people who put them down and put them in their places. That's how bullies win. That's the time, more than ever, that a person needs to get back up on the ladder of success!

Work on self-esteem. After that, you can worry about the success. If you can't feel good about yourself, you're in trouble. How is somebody else going to feel about you if you feel like a zero? If you say, "I don't deserve it," then it won't happen. You have to get back to the mirror and start building that self-esteem. Start reminding yourself of the good and right things in your life.

M FOR Motivation!

"perfection is not attainable, but if we chase perfection, we can catch excellence."

~Vince Lombardi

You feel good about yourself when you do good and it's reinforced by people around you. Most people know right from wrong. You don't have positive self-esteem if you do wrong—the guilt will come into play. **When you do right, though, you feel good about what you're achieving.** You feel good about working in a job when people see how hard you work. Somebody will see you and give you a chance. **There's more good in the world than bad.** You'll break that barrier between the bottom rung of your ladder of success and the steps that will take you to your dream.

When you're going through a tough time, your self-worth is awful. That's an opening for anybody who wants to knock you down. It's up to you to keep your self-esteem strong so that you're too strong for bullies, for your own negative thoughts, or for society to knock you off of your ladder of success.

GAME TIPS!
Remember...

Move Past Bad Choices by Making New Good Choices

Success Can Only Be Built on a Foundation of Self-Esteem

The most precious gift anyone has is health. If you have that, you have half the battle beaten. Every day, mothers and fathers are sitting at bedsides from dawn to midnight while their children are battling illnesses. That's tough times. Everything else is just a detour. **Life is full of bumps and bruises.** When adversity strikes, such as: a person is fired, parents separate, there's an illness, the work is hard, or somebody seems to be blocking your way, you have to deal with it. Don't avoid it or let it break you. If you want a W in the game of life, dealing with the adversity is the *only* choice.

It won't go smoothly every day of your life, no matter who you are. I lost my eye and it was hard, but it didn't stop me. I lost my job and I thought that was the end, but

"Don't avoid adversity or let it break you."

it turned out to be the beginning. **You have to pick up the pieces of difficult times with *mental toughness*, and build a better you than you were before.**

Awesome, Baby with a Capital A!

Kurt Weiss was still a teenager when he began a fight against osteosarcoma, a very aggressive bone cancer. At the time, he was a fifteen-year-old lineman on his high school's football team and had dreams of attending Notre Dame like his sister before him. That's when an aching in his shin caused concern from his team trainer. His trainer made an appointment with Dr. Jack Failla of the Pittsburgh Pirates. That appointment led to more concern and an appointment the very next day that Kurt was told to "not be late" for. He never imagined when his mom took him to the doctor recommended by Dr. Failla that the doctor would discover a cancer that had already metastasized. In the depths of his war with the horrible illness, he underwent bone grafts, surgery, and chemotherapy, but the disease kept spreading. It spread to his lungs. It was spreading in the midst of his chemo treatments, which is a pretty sure sign that the treatments aren't working at all. During the worst of the suffering, cancer had taken up residence in Kurt's leg and forced him to have a graft that eventually became infected, causing the amputation of his leg. Kurt even became a "wish kid" through the Make a Wish Foundation (an organization he still supports today). His wish? He knew he couldn't play football for the school he once dreamed about, but he wanted to march onto the field with the Notre Dame marching band. Not only did Kurt have his wish fulfilled and march with the Fighting Irish, he would be back! His journey is what makes Kurt one of the miracles. **His story is one of the reasons that the V Foundation for Cancer Research continues to do**

what it does. It raises money to help people fight cancer on the front lines like Kurt Weiss. Kurt didn't succumb to cancer. When almost all hope was lost, his sister found an article on an experimental immunotherapy. **Kurt figured that if he was going to die, he was at least going to make sure something could be learned from it.** As it turned out, the treatment was successful and Kurt was able to claim that he had been through everything with the disease... except his own death. Instead of taking his recovery easy, the future Dr. Weiss returned to Notre Dame, this time as a student. He continued in band and even led it, on his one leg, in his senior year. Kurt was a valuable asset to the Notre Dame Fighting Irish Marching Band during the Orange Bowl—an extension of his wish that he never imagined. That perseverance, that undefeatable attitude to reach his dream despite incredible adversity, is what led Kurt, after becoming cancer-free, to continue working against the illness. After he beat the odds against osteosarcoma, he became an orthopedic surgeon at the University of Pittsburgh, even studying at one time under the very doctor who oversaw his own experimental treatment. Kurt Weiss is today working as a musculoskelatal oncologist to beat the very cancer that almost killed him. When he spoke at my V Foundation for Cancer Research gala, he was so passionate and so inspiring that he brought the house to its feet. I told the people at the gala, "I want those research dollars in the hands of people like Dr. Kurt Weiss!" Moments after his speech, donations to the V Foundation for Cancer Research increased. Dr. Weiss didn't just use mental toughness to beat his own cancer; he used it to build a career in beating the disease out of the next generation of patients. For his incredible feats in the battle against cancer, Kurt Weiss is absolutely *Awesome, Baby, with a Capital A!*

Just a few years into my career with ESPN, the University of Houston Cougars path to the NCAA men's basketball championship was strong. The soon-to-be NBA Hall of Famer, Clyde Drexler, was confident. His future fellow Naismith Hall of Famer, Hakeem Olajuwon, towered above the competition. Those two weren't the whole story. The entire team was great... even the names you don't remember. Head Coach Guy Lewis was closing in on thirty brilliant years with the Cougars. This is the Guy who finally, fabulously coached in five final fours. The University of Houston players made up a multi-talented team—the Phi Slama Jama* of men's basketball. They were the athletic, high-flying, dazzling, dunking, number-one pick across the nation for the 1982-1983 season. They went into the NCAA championship game with only two losses.

The interesting thing, though, is that the drama wasn't theirs. This game would be all about the underdog—the under-wolf. I'm talking about the Heart Attack Pack*. I'm talking about the Cardiac Kids*. I'm talking about the buzzer-beating North Carolina State Wolfpack under Head Coach Jimmy Valvano. The Wolfpack was the real tale that year—the Cinderella story.

The Pack's climb wasn't as secure as the Cougars'. They went into the post-season with ten losses, but

*From Dickie V's DicKtionary

Phi Slama Jama— the nickname given to the Houston Cougars because of their amazing ability to dunk the basketball.

Heart Attack Pack or Cardiac Kids— the nickname given to the North Carolina State Wolfpack who often won games in comeback fashion, keeping fans on the edge of their seats.

Jimmy V said, "Never give up." The Pack was behind in one game, but he said, "Never give up." Again and again, the pack was behind and their coach said, "Never give up."

FROM tHe

File

M FOR Motivation!

"Never give up."

~Jim Valvano

Five games in the NCAA tournament had the Wolfpack losing early, and five games they came out winners! Five from-behind games, Baby! They took every one of them in true cardiac fashion! They took them because they didn't believe in "can't," they didn't have a fear of failure, and they NEVER gave up!

The Wolfpack climbed for Jimmy Valvano, whom they loved. They worked hard; they scratched and clawed their way up to that championship game against the kings of the dunk, the assumed champion Houston Cougars. The Wolfpack climbed straight to Albuquerque, which was a real climb, I'm telling you. That year, the championship game was held in that high-altitude city of New Mexico which is very difficult on an athlete. I'm telling you the air was thin that night. The only way the Pack had a chance to stop this juggernaut was to control the tempo of the game. Fans were frenzied in the stands. It was fabulous!

At the half, Jimmy's team was up by 8, but the lead would dwindle soon. I remember Jimmy's face when his team missed the first shot of the second half. Then they missed another shot... they missed again. Nine times—nine times they missed! The lead was gone. The pack was down by 7. They were written off. Fans were echoing in the stands that they were surprised North Carolina State had hung in as long as they did.

Fans didn't realize that the Wolfpack had Jimmy's advice ringing in their ears. They were ready to turn up the mental toughness when their bodies were nearly spent. At last, they made a shot and the Cardiac Kids started the thumping of the heart in their coach's chest.

Jimmy's expression returned back to hopeful. The Cougars' lead began to shrink. Jimmy V had his Pack controlling the tempo of the game and converting from Area Code J*!

Finally, the tying shot flew through the air. It was Awesome, Baby! The NCAA championship game was tied with less than two minutes to go! Jimmy couldn't sit still. Now, it was Maalox Masher* time for Guy Lewis. His stomach was beginning to churn as he wiped his face with his red and white towel. The crowd chants changed from "HOUSTON" to "STATE!" and State climbed. They climbed. They never gave up! Two seconds were left in the game! Then came

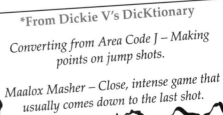

*From Dickie V's DicKtionary

Converting from Area Code J – Making points on jump shots.

Maalox Masher – Close, intense game that usually comes down to the last shot.

a shot from thirty feet back for State's Dereck Whittenburg and it was an Airball, Baby! AIRBALL… it fell short.

No way! No way was NC State going to quit this close to the finish. It was time for another player to climb, Lorenzo Charles. He hadn't made a shot in the second half. He climbed. He climbed. He became a skywalker*! He wanted that ball at crunch time*. And the shot that didn't go long enough? He got a hold of it with a SLAM! BAM! JAM!* 54 to 52 at the buzzer, Charles out-dunked the Phi Slama Jama to take the whole thing with his team! They never gave up; they climbed to the championship; they climbed to the last shot, and then—victory in their hands—they climbed the basket itself and stood on top of the world while Jimmy V ran back and forth on the court in disbelief, looking for somebody to hug.

Dick interviews Jimmy V after an NC State win.

It was the greatest moment in basketball history I've ever witnessed.

Valvano didn't end up on top of the world by chance. He spent a lot of years working hard and being mentally tough. He was coaching nineteen-year-olds in basketball when he was only twenty-one, himself. He worked in PRIDE (passion, respect, intelligence, determination, and enthusiasm) his whole life to make his basketball coaching dreams come true. Jimmy worked at beating the odds again and again. He beat those odds when

*From Dickie V's DicKtionary

Skywalker – a good leaper.

Crunch Time – the time in a game (or the game of life) that matters the most and will make a difference in the win or loss.

Slam! Bam! Jam! – an impressive slam dunk

he was an underdog coach taking championships and he beat the odds by keeping a great attitude when life got hard.

Jimmy kept a commitment to excellence and kept his dreams alive despite any problem he was facing, and he faced struggles far greater than basketball games. What was important to him was spending some time thinking about where he started, where he was, and where he was going. It was easy for him to see where he'd been because he carried around little white index cards that had all of his goals written on them. Over the years, he was able to cross off goal after goal because he made them happen. Then came the goal he never wanted to set.

FROM tHE M FiLE

M FOR Motivation!

"Spend some time thinking about where you started, where you are, and where you're going to be."

~Jim Valvano

Jimmy V was told he had cancer and it was going to claim his life in less than a year. It was the toughest opponent ever for the champion, so he wanted to help end the awful disease for as many people as possible. He said it was the only good he could possibly see in it, the only good that could come from his suffering. Against the odds, in his most difficult struggle, he was looking for good and inspiring others! Even when his body was riddled with cancer, he was telling his friends and family—his TEAM—the important things from life that carry on after a person is gone. He didn't mention basketball.

A month and a half before he died, Jimmy gave an inspirational speech as the first-ever recipient of the Arthur Ashe Courage Award*. Along with Mike Krzyzewski and NFL legend, Joe Theismann, I helped my friend to the stage. Earlier that day, we weren't sure Jimmy would be well enough to accept the award. He had to use a morphine pump to tolerate the pain. Once on stage, though, he was the motivating, elevating, great man so many of us were blessed to know.

As the producers for the awards show tried repeatedly to get Jimmy Valvano to wrap it up, he defiantly waved them off because he knew he had something important to tell us and to tell the generations that wouldn't be lucky enough to know the man in person. He knew this would be his last chance to say what he needed to say. I

*From Dickie V's DicKtionary

Arthur Ashe Courage Award – named for Arthur Ashe (African American tennis superstar who died in 1993 from AIDS contracted through a blood transfusion), this award is given annually (since 1993) to individuals who transcend sports by showing courage and a "never give up" attitude in life outside of sports. The award was inspired by a courageous life on and off the tennis courts and embodied in one of Ashe's own quotations: "Every time you win, it diminishes the fear a little bit. You never really cancel the fear of losing; you keep challenging it."

wasn't the only one crying when he powerfully shared the wisdom that comes through life struggles if you are mentally tough.

"There are three things we all should do every day. We should laugh every day. We should spend some time in thought. We should have our emotions moved to tears— it could be from happiness or joy, too. If we laugh, we think, and we cry, that's a full day. That's a heckuva day."

You see, Jimmy's body may have had cancer, but not his heart, his mind, and his soul. He ended his speech with the same spirit of the underdog he used to lead the Cardiac Pack to victory ten years earlier, saying, "Don't give up. Don't ever give up."

That new goal my friend had written was found by his wife, Pam, after Valvano's passing. It was on another index card in the pocket of a sport coat. He wanted to learn how to paint, play piano, and find a cure for cancer. His family and friends are working hard to cross that last goal off of his index card for him. His own daughter became a breast cancer survivor, and, through the V Foundation for Cancer Research, cancer patients all over the country have Coach Jimmy V in their corners. My friend's legacy is not the cutting down of the nets at the 1983 NCAA Championship game, but the many people he will affect in generation after generation with the millions of dollars raised in his name. Jimmy V would be smiling to

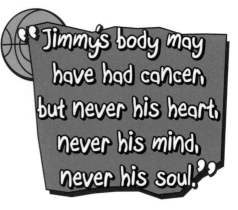

know that the V-Foundation for Cancer Research has raised over $120 Million Dollars for cancer research.

Jimmy would be so proud knowing that one of his championship players from that all-time great historical basketball game, Dereck Whittenburg, is on the board of the V Foundation for Cancer Research. He's done an amazing job raising money on behalf of and in the spirit of his former coach. Jimmy touched lives on and off the court and continues to do so. What makes a person a hero isn't what they do on the athletic courts of life, but in the game of life. Jimmy owned every moment of his life and captained it with PRIDE and undeniable MENTAL TOUGHNESS. For that, Jimmy Valvano will always remain my hero.

VSTARS

James (Jimmy V) Thomas Anthony Valvano

- Wrote down goals.
- Was mentally tough.
- Committed to excellence.
- Inspired the V Foundation for Cancer Research.

Making MENTAL TOUGHNESS work for you!

Winning is the ability of an individual—in pursuit of any goal or dream—to do his or her best. It's not the ability to do your best when everything is going well. It's not the ability to do your best when everybody likes you, when people speak gently to you, or when you have the support of the world. Winning is doing your best always and in the face of every adversity—physical, mental, or spiritual—that you encounter.

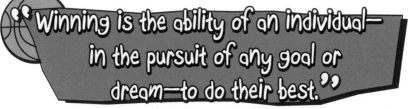

"Winning is the ability of an individual— in the pursuit of any goal or dream—to do their best."

Think of a time when you did not achieve a goal. It could be an athletic win, a grade in a class or on a paper, or earning your way toward a reward.

What positive lesson can you take away from *not* reaching a specific goal you set?

_____

_____

Whether it is from you, from your TEAM, from your rivals, or from society, there are always expectations you hope to meet in pursuit of your goals. Ultimately, as long as those expectations are in line with making good and right decisions and avoiding doing wrong, you will maintain your support system, your self-esteem, and the upward climb toward your dream.

In pursuit of your goals, what expectations do YOU have about...

The right things I need to do:

_____

_____

A wrong choice I need to avoid:

_____

_____

Does this differ from the expectations of your TEAM?

_____

_____

Does this differ from the expectations of your rivals?

_____

_____

Does this differ from the expectations of society?

_____

_____

We cannot control the opinions of others, but we can control our own performance in tasks related to our goals.

What long-term research do you need to study in pursuit of your goal?

_____

_____

_____

What short-term preparation do you need at each step of your goal?

_____

_____

_____

There are things you will do as you chase your dreams that aren't related to your ultimate goal. I learned work ethic from watching my dad in a job I knew I would never have. Think about a job or activity you've had that could prove helpful.

What lesson did you learn from a task not related to your own goal?

_____

_____

As we learned through the stories of Larry Bird and Earvin "Magic" Johnson, even your rivals can support you if you earn their respect through hard work.

What do you do on your ladder of success that you think should earn the respect of your rivals?

_____

_____

What is something admirable you've seen in one of your rivals?

_____

_____

> *Throughout our discussions on mental toughness, we discovered that bullying comes in many forms and from many fronts. Regardless of where you are forced to confront bullying, defeat it with self-esteem, positive thinking and living.*

Are you your biggest bully? What negative self-talk are you starting to believe about yourself (and do you vow to defeat that negativity?)?

_____

_____

Bullies make us focus on those negatives and those "failures." Think about some of your successes. List three of them here:

1. _____

2. _____

3. _____

What T.E.A.M. building action items from **MENTAL TOUGHNESS** will you *take possession* of in your life with *desire, dedication, determination, and discipline (the D's in PRIDE)?* See my mental toughness **playbook** at the end of this book section for hints!

_____

_____

_____

_____

You can fool the world down the pathway
   of years
And get pats on the back as you pass,
But your final reward will be heartaches
   and tears,
If you've cheated the guy in the glass.
                    ~From: Dale Wimbrow's
                       "The Guy in the Glass"

CaN't CoN tHe MiRRoR

When we spoke about **Togetherness**, we discovered that you have to be comfortable with what you put out into the world in terms of social media. Are you representing yourself as the real you? We talked about defining yourself (rather than defending yourself) in our discussions on **Enthusiasm**. When Leslie Cason spoke to Ian O'Connor about what drugs did to his life, during our **Attitude** portion of the T.E.A.M. model, he told the reporter that the only person to blame was, ". . . the man in the mirror." Using **Mental Toughness**, my daughter, Terri, faced the mirror every day to remind herself that she belonged on her road to success while at Notre Dame.

You can't con the mirror. You can con your coach. You can con your folks. You can con other people, but you can't

con the mirror because that mirror looks right back at you. If you're guilty, that head will go down.

Tear out the next page and cut out the center frame. Tape this to a mirror you see every day. Who do you see? Do you see somebody being bullied or somebody with strong self-esteem? Do you see somebody who quits when facing adversity or do you see somebody who is ready, willing, and able to make TEAM work for YOU on your path to getting a W in the game of life?

Practice your Can't Con the Mirror activity every night by facing yourself and asking questions about your day. It is your genuine "time of reflection." If you can do something every single day that makes you a better person than you were the day before, then you're gonna be *Awesome, Baby, with a Capital A!*

Ask yourself:

Was I really prepared today to do the best I could possibly do?

Did I look at my checklist of my daily goals and did I achieve them?

If not, will I attack them tomorrow?

What did I do today to make me a better person than I was yesterday?

Cut out

Did I read about successful people and what made them a success?

What steps did I take today to advance in quest of my goals and dreams?

How can I be better tomorrow?

"YOU CAN'T CON THE MIRROR!"

~DICK VITALE

DICKIE V'S MENTAL TOUGHNESS PLAYBOOK
MOTIVATE by defeating expectations...

Enjoy the anticipation at the start of your journey toward your goal.

Develop a winner's edge.

Don't mix your expectations up with the expectations of the world.

Have long-term research goals and short-term preparation goals.

Don't hold yourself back because of lower expectations from the world.

Mental Toughness begins with the right mental state.

Don't be held back from your best efforts because of weak excuses.

Don't try to enjoy the fruits of your labor before you put in the labor.

Labor and fitness have results that go far beyond appearance.

Don't disrespect physical efforts.

Preparation is the key to success.

Exert the effort needed to reach your goals.

Be punctual to earn the respect of your leaders and your equals.

Get an education.

Make good choices about your health and fitness.

Don't ignore the lessons of those who have different life paths than you.

Don't just scrape by on natural ability.

If you strive for perfection, you will be able to achieve excellence.

Spend some time thinking about your beginnings, your present, and your future.

Be prepared to do your best each day.

Look daily at your checklist of goals.

Attack goals tomorrow that you haven't achieved today.

Do something every day to make you a better person.

Read about successful people.

Take steps to advance toward your goal every day.

Always plan to be a better total person tomorrow.

ELEVATE by defeating bullies...

Learn to deal with all different types of leaders, mentors, and bosses.

Work hard no matter how you're being asked to do that work.

Don't let hurt feelings stop progress.

Don't crumble under the pressure of criticism.

Learn to handle all types of communicators; have good people skills.

Appreciate the power of excellence.

Don't allow self-pity to rule you.

Succeed because of your abilities and your efforts.

Always work to improve yourself.

Believe in the willingness of your TEAM to have your back.

You are more than your appearance.

Don't allow your looks to dictate your self-esteem.

Be beautiful in your heart, your mindset, and your life.

Learn how to be a good person.

Self-esteem should be built on knowing a total person.

Isolate emotional drains and keep them out of your life.

Bullying is weak.

Beat bullying back with your strength of mind... your mental toughness.

Keep bad choices off your life resume.

Face bullying head-on.

Don't beat yourself up over mistakes—everybody makes them.

Work on your self-esteem.

When you do right, you feel good about what you're achieving.

There's more good in the world than bad.

Move past bad choices by making new, good choices.

Success can only be built on a foundation of good self-esteem.

You can't con the mirror.

BE GREAT by defeating your quitter...

Don't quit.

Do not have a fear of failure.

Don't walk away from your goal when it gets hard.

Enjoy the rewards of hard work.

Punctuality matters.

Effort matters.

Strong work ethic means security in the job you have.

Work, education, discipline and determination can make your dream a reality.

If you show a willingness to work hard to reach your dream, then your support system won't be far behind.

A winner's work is never done.

Give your all—all the time.

Match the efforts of your rivals.

Don't allow excuses to hold you back from your best.

Don't be afraid of a little discomfort when it could help you succeed.

Don't expect the easy road to be the road to success.

Accept that you're going to have setbacks in life.

Look at failure as a stepping stone.

Don't shy away from physical labor.

There is no "off-season" when it comes to chasing your dream.

Failures are just setbacks.

Don't allow excuses to stop you from attempting your dreams.

Don't let failures be dead-ends.

Don't avoid adversity or let it break you.

Pick up the pieces after difficult times and use them to build a better you.

Don't let adversity pollute your mind, your heart, or your spirit.

Do your best in the pursuit of your dream and despite any adversity.

NEVER GIVE UP!

YOU'RE GONNA BE AWESOME, BABY!

Dick enjoys the energy building in the stands before a game.

Dick enjoys a day with young boys in conversations and on the court.

The Post-Game

Motivate, Elevate, and Be Great!

Put your TEAM to work...

I've shared a lot in these pages and it hasn't been just advice I want to give you, although I hope you've found a few valuable nuggets. These aren't just stories of super-stars with natural talent who went on to make millions, although I know a few guys who happen to fit that mold.

These are stories of great successes that occurred because of great relationships, great choices, and great attitudes. These pages weren't meant to lecture—they were meant to love.

Every day, my wife and I feel blessed to wake up in the life we have, and it has nothing to do with fame or fortune. It has to do with the TOGETHERNESS we've built with family, friends, colleagues, and everybody we meet. We face each day with ENTHUSIASM, defining ourselves and our lives by it. We try to have a positive ATTITUDE to build the energy needed to be confident in our right choices. We experience MENTAL TOUGHNESS by getting back in the game of life after setbacks and by supporting those who have true adversity through life situations such as illness.

I feel that we have a W in the game of life. It came not by accident, but by following this T.E.A.M. model. It's a formula I passionately desire to share with young people everywhere. I want you to know that success can happen for anybody with any background if you plan, pursue, and persevere. We *will* be a TEAM; you *can* earn a W in the game of life, and you're gonna be *Awesome, Baby, with a Capital A*!

Tear Out and Keep

Get Your W in the Game of Life!
~Dickie V

The T.E.A.M. Model

✂ Tear Out and Keep

T.ogetherness
E.nthusiasm
A.ttitude
M.ental Toughness

DiCKie V's DiCKtioNaRY
Terms from "Vitalese" and from the Game of Life

ACC: Atlantic Coast Conference, one of the elite NCAA conferences in college athletics.

Airball: a basketball shot that misses the basket so thoroughly, it hits nothing but air.

Area Code J: to convert from here is to make points on long jump shots.

Arthur Ashe Courage Award: named for Arthur Ashe (African American tennis superstar who died in 1993 from AIDS contracted through a blood transfusion), this award is given annually (since 1993) to individuals who transcend sports by showing courage and a "never give up" attitude in life outside of sports.

Attitude: the taste for success and the desire to attain it despite any obstacle.

Bucket List: a list of goals or activities to do before you die.

Cardiac Kids: *(see heart attack pack)* - the nickname given to the North Carolina State Wolfpack who often won games in comeback fashion, keeping fans on the edge of their seats.

Crunch-time: the time in a game (or the game of life) that matters the most and will make a difference in the win or loss.

Diaper Dandy: a "Vitalese" term; a great basketball player who is only a freshman.

Dipsy-do Dunk-a-roo: a "Vitalese" term; a fancy slam dunk.

Dish the Rock: a "Vitalese" term; pass the ball.

Dow Joneser: a "Vitalese" term; an inconsistent player; an up and down player.

Elevate: to raise to a higher level.

Enthusiasm: when people approach activities with this emotion, they uplift those they work with in any phase of life.

Final Four: the games remaining between the last four teams competing in the NCAA elimination-style championship tournament.

Five-star player: a big-time player who could play anywhere in the nation.

Given the Ziggy: fired.

Greatness: when individuals consistently do their best through right living and good choices.

Harlem Globetrotters: beginning in 1926, this basketball team is all about showmanship, putting on a display of great games and great tricks with the basketball.

Heart Attack Pack: *(see cardiac kids)* the nickname given to the North Carolina State Wolfpack who often won games in comeback fashion, keeping fans on the edge of their seats.

Holiday Festival Tournament: an All-Star basketball event for college teams.

Kazaam: a genie character that Shaquille O'Neil played in a family friendly movie in 1996.

Maalox Masher: Close, intense game that usually comes down to the last shot.

Mental Toughness: what winners show in difficult times, when faced with adversity, and when the going is tough.

Motivate: to be inspired to move in a forward or an upward motion.

No-hitter: a magical moment for a pitcher when he completes the game without allowing a base hit.

Paraphernalia: usually referring specifically to illegal drugs, this refers to any of the tools necessary to using those drugs including, but not limited to, injection needles.

Phi Slama Jama: the nickname given to the Houston Cougars because of their amazing ability to dunk the basketball.

PTPer: a "Vitalese" term; Prime-Time Player; a player of great basketball skill.

Shut down/Shut out: a game in which the losing team does not score against the winner.

Skywalker: a good leaper.

Slam! Bam! Jam!: an impressive slam dunk

SRO: standing room only; a sign that goes go up on the entrances of sold-out events.

Success: meeting your goals through passion, hard work, and intelligent decisions.

Sweet 16: in college basketball, this refers to the top sixteen teams that are fighting their way toward the NCAA championship title game in a bracket-style elimination playoff.

T.E.A.M. Model: Dick Vitale's model for success including togetherness, enthusiasm, attitude, and mental toughness.

Team: a group of people, often in athletic events, striving to reach a single goal or victory.

TEAM: your life team built with all the people who help you on your ladder of success.

Three-star player: a mid-major college basketball player.

Togetherness: when people function and work as a team; a blending of people of different races and backgrounds.

Trifecta: a "Vitalese" term; a three-point basket.

Upset: when three-star players play well enough to beat a team of mostly five-star players.

Winner: any individual who, in the pursuit of a goal or dream, does his or her best.

INDEX OF TEAM TOPICS

TEAM Roster
Featured People in "Getting a W in the Game of Life"

Acknowledgements

Special thanks are due to so many without whom this book would not have been possible. Lorraine Vitale, Terri Sforzo, and Sherri Krug, your support, kindness, and input throughout this project have been a blessing. To Joe Laberge, your passion for this book has been greatly appreciated.

Susan Lipton, the value of your support and cheerleading of this and all Vitale projects cannot be understated. We would also like to acknowledge Howie Schwab for his dedicated assistance.

To Bob Snodgrass, Publisher at Ascend Books, thank you for believing in this project and especially for believing in those who helped put it together.

Thank you also to Chris Drummond, Publication Coordinator at Ascend Books, for keeping us on task.

Much appreciation for Bob Ibach, Rob Peters, Blake Hughes, and all of those at Ascend Books who made "Getting a W" happen.

This couldn't have been done without the keen editorial eye of Stacy Rozmarynowski. Also, for providing invaluable input, thank you to Mike Tirico, George Raveling, Bob Stolarz, Tom Crean, John Saunders, Mike Krzyzewski, Rick Pitino, George Bodenheimer, Billy Donovan, John Calipari, and Lou Ravettine.

A debt of gratitude is owed to Brandon Stephenson, Andy Averill, and their Slife and Edge youth groups who provided priceless insights into the concerns and questions of today's young men and young ladies. I'd also like to add a special shout-out to Reji's three children, Bradley, Kimberly, and Laura, who were often tapped for youth opinions and perspectives.

Lastly, to the many whose life stories inspired this playbook for life, it is your lessons, lived by example, that are helping to provide a blueprint for success sure to inspire the next generation.

You're all Awesome, Baby, with a Capital A!

ABOut tHe AutHORs

Dick Vitale has been ESPN's voice of Men's College Basketball since 1979. Eleven Halls of Fame and countless heartfelt recognitions have affirmed the passionate vitality he brings to sports broadcasting make an equal impact on raising millions of dollars for pediatric cancer research through the V Foundation for Cancer Research. He is as much a household name for his humanitarian deeds as he is for the game he loves. Dick has been working for many years sharing the motivational life tips he believes in and succeeds by with everyone from major firms to small youth groups. Nobody is better suited to enthusiastically teach winning in life than Dickie V. Dick is the author of nine books including *"Dick Vitale's Fabulous 50 Moments and Players"* and *"Dickie V's ABC's and 1-2-3's."* Dick lives with his wife, Lorraine, in Florida. They have two daughters and five grandchildren. Learn more at **www.dickvitaleonline.com**.

Reji Laberje is a writer and speaker who has presented entertaining, educational programs to thousands of students since 1997. She's the author of e-books, audio books, and six books, including *"The Tale Travelers"* series and *"Cooper Ridge, The Wonder Kid"*. With three children of her own, she's thrilled to be a part of Dick's positive living playbook. Reji lives with her husband of 16 years, Joe, near Milwaukee, Wisconsin. Learn more at **www.rejilaberje.com**.

Photo Courtesy Bob Snodgrass

Dick Vitale with co-author, Reji Laberje, at the Broken Egg in Sarasota, Florida.